Growing Up: From eight years to young adulthood

Jennie Lindon

The National Children's Bureau was established as a registered charity in 1963. Our purpose is to identify and to promote the interests of all children and young people and to improve their status in a diverse society.

We work closely with professionals and policy makers to improve the lives of all children but especially young children, those affected by family instability, children with special needs or disabilities and those suffering the effects of poverty and deprivation.

We collect and disseminate information about children and promote good practice in children's services through research, policy and practice development, publications, seminars, training and an extensive library and information service.

The Bureau works in partnership with Children in Scotland and Children in Wales.

© National Children's Bureau, 1996

ISBN 1 874579 61 X

Published by National Children's Bureau Enterprises Ltd, 8 Wakley Street, London EC1V 7QE. Telephone 0171 843 6000.

National Children's Bureau Enterprises is the trading company for the National Children's Bureau (Registered Charity number 258825).

Typeset by Books Unlimited (Nottm), NG19 7QZ

Printed and bound in the United Kingdom by Biddles Ltd

Contents

Photographers' credits

Acknowledgements

The content of this book has benefited enormously from the suggestions, opinions and experiences offered by others. I would specifically like to thank the following people who read the first draft of the book and offered constructive feedback:

- Sheryl Burton, Practice Development Department, National Children's Bureau
- John Coleman, Trust for the Study of Adolescence
- Liz Cowley, Early Childhood Unit, National Children's Bureau
- Erica De'Ath, Stepfamily
- Gerison Lansdown, Children's Rights Office
- John Metcalfe, Department of Health
- Gillian Pugh, Early Childhood Unit, National Children's Bureau
- Debi Roker, Trust for the Study of Adolescence
- Philippa Russell OBE, Council for Disabled Children
- Dorothy Selleck, Early Childhood Unit, National Children's Bureau
- Ruth Sinclair, Research Department, National Children's Bureau
- Celia Smith, Research Department, National Children's Bureau
- Olivia Vincenti, London Borough of Barnet
- Lesley Waldron, student
- Phil Youdan, Children's Residential Care Unit, National Children's Bureau

I would like to thank the many children and young people who have expressed their views and answered my questions during individual conversations over the years. I wish specifically to thank my son, Drew and daughter, Tanith, for their help – deliberate and more unwitting. They have helped me to build a bridge between research on children and young people and how everyday life works in practice.

During the summer term of 1995 I was given invaluable help by three schools who gave me the opportunity to run informal discussions with their pupils. I would like to thank:

- Ravenstone Primary School in South London for the groups of Year 5 and 6 children (ten- and 11-year-olds).

- The Angmering School, West Sussex for groups of Year 7, 8, 9 and 12 (pupils of 12, 13, 14 and 17 years of age).
- Burntwood School in South London for Years 8 and 12 (13 and 17 years of age).

I also appreciate the time given for conversation by many adults within my personal and professional networks. They have shared their more recent experiences with children and young people, as well as recollections of their own youth. Their honesty has supported the attempt to blend research information with individual examples.

As author, I take the usual responsibility for the final form of the book, the particular way of expressing the ideas and information, and for decisions about the content and balance.

The research for and the writing of this book was made possible by a grant from the Department for Health's Parenting Initiative.

Introduction

The aims of this book

The book has three main aims. These are:

- *To describe the main changes that happen to children and young people as they make the move from middle childhood to the brink of adulthood.*

  All children and young people do not, of course, follow identical patterns through these years. Yet there are some consistent themes that affect everyone – in one way or another. Much of this material is drawn from research, surveys and smaller scale studies of older children and young people.

- *To set the changing experiences from approximately eight to 18 years within a practical and positive framework, illustrated by the viewpoints of children and young people themselves.*

  Research can be very informative but sometimes deals with different aspects of development as if they operate completely separately. The honestly expressed views of children and young people can bring such research data to life.

  The perspectives of children and young people tend to contrast with those who are currently adults, but do not necessarily conflict. The different outlook is a timely reminder that life usually does not look the same when you are 14 years old, as when you are 40.

  The material within the book to meet this aim is drawn partly from studies that have gathered the views of young people. The quoted material within the book is taken from many conversations with children, young people and adults, and from the school groups thanked in the acknowledgements.

- *To offer fresh perspectives and practical suggestions to adults who are concerned with older children and young people.*

  One aim is to inform readers and to refresh their knowledge. However, an equally important aim is to encourage adults to reflect on how they think about children and young people, and to consider other possible viewpoints from what appears to be the more obvious angle or explanation.

If adults are to be genuinely helpful to children and young people, then they need to acknowledge and try to understand the perspective of younger people. It is unreasonable to require that the understanding, or acceptance, only travels in the opposite direction.

Readers of the book

The book is written for adults who are involved with older children and young people. You will find the book useful if:

- *You are a parent of a child approaching this age range or already within the span of eight to 18 years.*

  The book will be equally relevant if you are caring for older children and young people as a relative or foster parent. The information and ideas within the book will help you to look afresh at what is happening to the children whom you know personally. New perspectives can help you to make some sense of the impact of changes on you and your life with the children or young people.

- *You are professionally involved with children in this age group or their families.*

  The book focuses on the children and young people themselves, rather than on different professional settings. This approach offers the advantage of a broader perspective than your specific professional interest or concern with children, young people or their families.

  You might be a teacher, a youth worker, or employed within the police or the probation services. Alternatively you could find the book useful if you are a social worker, a nurse in an adolescent unit or a worker in a residential home.

  Even very experienced workers will benefit from refreshing their knowledge of development and reflecting on what the changes mean for young people and those closely involved with them.

- *You are involved in parent education and support, or in training and advising any of the professional groups.*

  You will also find the book a resource on information and perspectives if you are working to help others to gain insight and understanding of children and young people.

Using the book

It is possible to read this book straight through in the order that it has been arranged. However, the content has been organised with the intention of making it easy for readers to move around sections, as their interest takes them. There are cross references between sections, when ideas or information naturally link together. The contents page provides a guide to the topics covered in each part of the book. The index will help readers who are interested in a particular issue or subject.

There are bound to be topics on which some readers would like more information. The Further reading section at the back of the book will be helpful in following up issues in greater detail. Within the text there are some specific suggestions for books that provide research reviews on complex or controversial topics. These references are all given in full in Further reading.

The context of this book

It is very difficult, probably impossible, to write a book of this kind unless an author recognises that the information and ideas are grounded in a particular place and time. Children and young people around the world have a very great deal in common. Yet, their development unfolds and they move towards maturity in very different societies, with varying expectations of both children and adults. The context of this book is, in time, the closing years of the twentieth century and, in place, the countries and diverse communities that make up a multiracial, multicultural and multilingual Britain.

Part one: Making sense of growing up

1. What is meant by growing up?

Growing up within a particular culture

The experience of children and young people can only make sense in terms of the society within which they are developing. Individuals do not grow from childhood into adulthood in a social vacuum. They experience the expectations of their close family and the more general messages of society as a whole. In turn, culture and tradition shape adult expectations of how children and young people should behave and should be treated.

Cultural or religious tradition within a society can influence adults' views, even when they feel they have moved away from their own family tradition, or are not active members of the religion that has most shaped their society. These messages and assumptions have been incorporated into everyday life in that society.

Learning values

Children come to understand the basic values of their own culture from an early age and can be more flexible than adults in learning new patterns, if they encounter different cultures. The key values that influence the behaviour and outlook of children, young people and adults are determined by the first culture within which they are raised.

It tends to be easier to identify the impact of culture for other families, who do not share one's own tradition. Most people tend to view their own culture and traditions as the normal way, and others as a deviation from what is usual or proper. Experience of other ways of running everyday life can make people think or provoke their interest. Unfortunately, the experience can also strengthen existing prejudices held by people within any cultural group.

Some broad differences

There can, of course, be considerable variation within cultures but traditions are established on the general issues of:

- What is more important – cooperation or competition? Are children

3

trained to stand out as the best or more to share the skills that they have?

- Appropriate behaviour towards a figure of authority, in the family or outside in the broader community. Is it polite to question or challenge such a figure?
- The appropriateness of assertiveness as an approach to others – whether this focuses on speaking one's mind or on personal needs and wishes.
- The importance of time, time-keeping and completing tasks fast.
- The place of individualism and personal rights, and the balance between this approach and obligations to family and society

The stance taken up on each of these broad issues exerts a strong influence on how children are raised and on how the educational process unfolds for them.

Admittedly, it is risky to attempt broad generalisations about cultures. However, Western European cultural traditions have tended to favour a competitive approach over genuine cooperation and an emphasis on speed rather than an outlook that some developments take time. There seems to have been a shift over the last few generations towards establishing a more individualistic tradition – for example, the concept of 'duty' will now sound old-fashioned to many ears.

The contrast in broad sweeps of basic values can become more obvious when several different cultures coexist within the same society, as is the situation in many European countries including Britain. Some children and young people, although able to develop a flexible outlook themselves, can find themselves torn, to a greater or lesser extent, when they are forced into making decisions over cultural loyalties.

Marking the move into adulthood

All cultures celebrate the move from child to adult, even when there is no single event or process that creates a rite of passage. In some cases, religious traditions provide a ritual to mark the move from childhood to adulthood. Some examples include the confirmation of 13- or 14-year-olds within the Church of England, the bar mitzvah ceremony for 13-year-old Jewish boys and the sacred thread ceremony, Upanyan, within the Hindu faith.

Sometimes, young people spend time away from the rest of the community, to return as accepted adults. The decision of some Western young people to spend weeks or months travelling beyond the bounds of Europe marks a similar boundary into adulthood. From the other side of the world, young people from Australia or New Zealand sometimes make the trip to Europe. The trips have an element of pleasure, but also a symbolic importance, since the young people are showing that they are sufficiently adult to organise and make a substantial journey.

Secular celebrations show that families and young people them-selves often want to mark the occasion of moving more into adulthood. This ritual is now the eighteenth birthday, but previously it was the twenty-first birthday that was the major turning point – known as 'getting the key to the door'. The shift came when the voting age was brought down from 21 to 18 years. Although the eighteenth birthday party may act as a symbol of leaving childhood, the legal framework of British society gives a confusing set of messages over when children are capable of taking on adult responsibilities (see page 6).

What is being 'grown up' in Britain?

In some societies, young people have to fulfil particular tasks or take on new responsibilities. They may be betrothed or married, or start to take on some of the work of adult family members. Around the world, and during previous decades in Britain, there have been differences in the age at which children are judged to be able to take on their adult role in society.

The boundaries to childhood

During this century, many European countries, including Britain, have stretched the years of childhood and blurred the boundary that marks the entry into adulthood. Childhood has tended to become defined in terms that the young people are:

- too young to work;
- still involved in formal education;
- involved in play and leisure activities that are separate from adult interests and responsibilities.

Such a working definition can leave large and physically mature 15- and 16-year-olds in an in-between stage, and often feeling that adults are inconsistent. For instance, some parents and teachers use phrases such as 'Grow up!' or 'Act your age' as a form of criticism. Yet the same young people may find that, in different circumstances, their plans are turned down on the grounds of, 'You're not old enough yet'.

It seems very likely that, in Britain, children and young people receive conflicting messages from adults, because the adults themselves are confused. For instance, today's 14-year-olds are frequently regarded as still partly children, yet some will have grandparents who left school and started work at that age. Despite their being some years away from many of the official milestones of adulthood, a great deal is still expected of 14-year-olds now. For example:

- Within their school work they are expected to be able to deal with some very complex ideas, to organise themselves to deal with a large work load and to manage the competing attractions of study and leisure time.
- In family and social life 14-year-olds are often expected to show a sense of responsibility by seeing things through and fulfilling their commitments.
- It is expected that 14-year-olds will resolve difficult situations with their friends and handle everyday conflicts.
- Despite the official view that they are still mainly children, some young people of 14 years are taking on a great deal of domestic responsibility when siblings or parents are seriously ill or disabled.

Growing up and the law

Legal milestones in England and Wales

Young people are adults in the eyes of the law when they pass their eighteenth birthday. Yet there are steps along the way that create a confusing picture over when young people are mature and responsible. British 16-year-olds can, for example:

- leave school;
- marry;
- have heterosexual sex;
- insist on confidentiality in medical consultations;
- enter military service;
- get a licence to drive a motor bike;
- join a trade union.

At 17 years' old, they are, additionally, able to:

- get a driving licence for a car;
- buy a firearm;
- hold a pilot's licence.

Yet, 17-year-olds still cannot own their own house or flat, serve on a jury or make a will. After their eighteenth birthday, they can legally drink alcohol in a public house; yet, because of a piece of legislation that has never been repealed, they have been able to drink at home, legally, since their fifth birthday. Two years after they are judged sufficiently responsible to fight and possibly die for their country, 18-year-olds are allowed to vote in elections and to take charge of their own finances, including gambling with their money. They can apply for credit cards, take out a mortgage and open the bank or building society accounts that were previously closed to them.

Legislation is introduced and then fine-tuned for a wide range of reasons, so it is perhaps not surprising that the legal framework does not give consistent messages over when individuals are no longer children. Changing legislation takes time and energy, so anomalies exist.

Of course, children and young people do not spend their leisure time leafing through various Acts of Parliament trying to work out when they are genuinely grown up in British society. Nor do they necessarily follow the letter of the law when they are aware of the facts. However, the various legal oddities are a reflection of confusion over when young people can be trusted to act in a fully adult manner. Perhaps the confusion for adults is just as great over what constitutes adult behaviour. If this is so, how can one judge when young people are definitely no longer children?

Children's rights

The UN Convention on the Rights of the Child

The United Nations Convention on the Rights of the Child was the first international treaty to recognise children's human rights as separate from and additional to those of adults. It came into force in 1990 and was signed by the UK government in 1991. The Convention is not part of UK domestic law; however, any legislation or administrative action should be compatible with the treaty, so the principles of the Convention can be used to raise concerns and to argue for children's rights. Up to 1995 the Convention had been ratified by 174 countries – a level of commitment that has exceeded any other international treaty.

The Convention set out basic principles for the treatment and status of children – under the age of 18 years – that apply across cultures and religions around the world. Article 12 is especially important since it explains the underlying principle that children who can express their views have the right to be heard and taken seriously. Adults should

listen to children's views about decisions in their lives and should take those views into consideration.

The meaning of children's rights

The focus on children's rights arose from a recognition that children are individuals whose views and feelings should be respected. They are not simply extensions of the adults, often parents, who are currently taking responsibility for their well-being. Individual children are growing all the time in their ability to express their own views and to contribute to decisions that affect their lives. Children's rights emphasises the obligation to make space within the family, schools, residential care and other services designed for children, to hear and allow properly for children's views and preferences.

A focus on children's rights does not lead to handing over all decisions to children. Nor is it a case of removing all rights or control from parents, or other adults such as teachers. The shift is one towards sharing control and making proper acknowledgement of the views of children and young people. Stressing children's rights does not inevitably weaken the rights of adults, although it will force a different perspective on adults who insist on very authoritarian control. The Children Act 1989 incorporated a view of parents' responsibilities towards their children, rather than their rights over them as if children were possessions.

Rights and responsibilities

Discussion of rights can never proceed in isolation. Stating the rights of one person, or a group of people inevitably moves to clarifying the responsibilities of others. This is as true of the family or school situation as in legal and national issues. Discussion of children's rights and adults' responsibilities leads naturally to consideration of the responsibilities of children and young people in the exercise of their rights. Perhaps here lies one of the key roles for concerned adults in supporting the process of growing up.

Is growing up different now?
'Young people today!'

Within any older generation there will always be some individuals who believe firmly that children and young people are failing to meet the impeccable standards met by the speakers when they were young. Complaints about 'young people today' can be found in writings of the ancient Greeks and Romans. Yet, successive generations have consistently managed to take over adult responsibilities and have then often discovered that the older generation were not quite as perfect as they had suggested.

Claims of irreconcilable differences between adults and young people – the so-called 'generation gap' – have also usually been much exaggerated. Children and young people certainly have disagreements with their parents (see page 103 for more discussion of this) but far more young people seem to accept their family's beliefs and standards than not. Studies that draw on reliable data for the views of previous generations of young people usually show that the values of many of the current younger generation are strikingly similar to their parents and, even, their grandparents. (For more on this topic readers could consult Cobb, 1992 or Coleman and Hendry, 1990.)

Viewpoint

Young people become understandably irritated and lose faith in adults who could be supportive when those adults appear to hold a totally different world view. This is not a new perspective for the current generation of young people. Looking back over their adolescent years, two men in their forties gave examples:

- 'When my first girlfriend threw me over, it was like my life had just stopped. And my parents said to me, "Don't worry, you'll be over it in no time. It's only puppy love." They lost all credibility in one go. It was the most important thing that had happened to me and they couldn't even see it.'
- 'I disliked school and it didn't get any better. My family had this cliché they would trot out about, "School days are the best years of your life." I thought it must be me, I'm the problem. And if these are the best years, what on earth is coming next!'

A question of respect

There are differences in perspective between the generations and one source of misunderstanding arises over the issue of respect.

Young people now are unlikely to accept that adults are owed respect solely on the basis of their additional years, their role as parent or grandparent, or their professional position, such as teacher. When young people are asked about this topic, they describe respect as something that adults earn, or lose, as a consequence of how they behave. The other side to this different perspective is that young people, and some older children, expect that they should receive respect from adults – for their opinions, efforts or hard work. They resent being on the receiving end of discourtesies that would be judged disrespectful if they were directed at an adult.

To think about

Conversations with honest adults, who are reflecting back over their schooldays, often reveal that previous generations of children did not have unquestioning respect for every teacher. Anecdotal evidence illustrates that teachers who were unkind, incompetent or inconsistent were not respected. Possibly, young people now express these feelings more openly.

The world of work

Possible unemployment

Previous generations did not all enjoy full employment, especially in some areas of the country. However, the pattern of employment or lack of it and the likely career pattern in jobs have changed. Young people now, even more than a decade ago, are having to prepare for an adulthood characterised by difficulties in getting a job – severe in some areas – changes of job and periods of unemployment. Families and schools are having to prepare young people for the realistic prospect that no job will be safe, even those professions which were once regarded as offering a secure career. The world of work has changed and young people have to be ready to learn new skills and think broadly about possible jobs. (More from page 174.)

Economic pressures can also affect children and young people through their parents' concerns about holding onto a job and earning sufficient for the family. Many parents are working long hours, with a consequent squeeze on time for the family.

Impact on leaving home

The difficulties of getting a job and the extended years of study undertaken by many young people can mean that they continue to be financially dependent on their parents. Even with a job, young adults may experience great difficulty in finding somewhere affordable to live and may have little option but to stay on in the family home.

In Britain the average age for leaving home in 1979 was 19 years. In 1990 this had risen to an average of 23 years. (These statistics can be found in *Social Trends*, 1992, collected by the Central Statistical Office.) This shift has implications for family relationships with adult sons and daughters. Parents would also be wise if they were to look ahead and encourage children progressively to become active members of the household, because that is a part of growing up, regardless of earning power.

Innovation in technology

Over the last 20 years there have been striking changes led by technological innovations. People have become accustomed to the wide range of bank and credit cards and to communication through mobile phones. Computer technology has become part of many jobs and has altered working life.

The changes of the last couple of decades have also transformed the kind of technology to be found in an ordinary home and therefore accessible to children and young people. There are advantages as well as potential disadvantages in this development. One consequence is that parents, who have not encountered computers within their work, can find themselves confused over technology that is utterly ordinary for their daughters and sons. (More on this from page 46.)

Marketing directed at children and young people

The previous generation of children and young people were targeted as possible buyers of toys, confectionery or clothes – or as effective naggers of the adults who did have money. However, the extent of the advertising onslaught has broadened, with saturation coverage within both television programming designed for children and young people and the increasing number of magazines targeted at children and young people. There has also been greatly increased use of television series and films as vehicles for promoting related merchandise.

This focus on purchase and possessions raises issues for parents in particular. They have to communicate, from their children's early childhood, the message that family finances are not bottomless and that people are more than what they own. Managing this lesson is part of teaching self reliance as children start to manage their own purchases with pocket money and later on their own finances. Some parents find refusing or re-directing their children's requests very difficult.

Young people's views on growing up

Older children and young people express opinions on the growing up process and their views reflect the different social messages that they receive. Individual conversations and the discussions undertaken for this book in three schools (thanked in the acknowledgements) provided some consistent themes. The 'you' in this section represents the children and young people who gave their views.

Growing up is not just about age

The general view was that you are not grown up at an exact age, although 16, or 18, is fairly much grown up. Part of being grown up is that you are larger and taller, but that is only seen as part of the process.

- 'It's not necessarily that you're big. It's how you act and talk, what you know. When you're an adult, you're 20 – out of your teens. Eighteen is a young adult.' (12-year-old)
- 'You're classed as an adult when you're 18, in terms of years. But you're a mature adult when people treat you like one, because you act that way.' (14-year-old)
- 'You could be mostly grown up and still live with your parents. Some 16- or 17-year-olds still go to school, or they can't get a job.' (10-year-old)
- 'It's silly. At 16 a girl can have a baby so why do people think that you're not completely grown up then?' (12-year-old)

Part of being grown up is what you can do

Children and young people generated a list of milestones that they felt were part of becoming grown up. It is a major change when you can do the following:

- leave school and your exams are all finished;
- earn money;
- go out with your friends wherever you like, without an adult;
- travel by yourself, perhaps to other countries;
- get the job that you want, be what you want to be;
- get married;
- own things like a car or a moped, your own home;
- see any film or video that you want, and the television programmes after 9.00 p.m.

What matters is how you behave

Children and young people point to the many different ways that more grown up people behave, summing them up using terms like 'sensible' or 'not immature'. They describe what they regard as more mature behaviour, although sometimes with the understanding that not all adults necessarily behave in that way all the time.

- 'You have more social skills. You think more about other people's feelings, how to treat other people. But you're still learning.' (14-year-old)
- 'It's how you look and the clothes that you wear.' (11-year-old)
- 'You deal with things yourself. You take responsibility for your actions.' (11-year-old)
- 'You're more tactful – like if somebody gives you something you don't like. If you're a child, then you say straight out, "I don't like that!" But when you're an adult, you find a more careful way to say it.' (11-year-old)
- 'It's when you're old enough to make your own decisions and some major decisions.' (12-year-old)
- 'You take responsibility for your actions. When you're younger, you might say, "It's wasn't me!"' (13-year-old)
- 'You get more serious, you have a serious side. You can still have a laugh, but without being pathetic. You can still find things funny.' (14-year-old)
- 'You deal with problems sensibly and rationally. With little children, they think about running away from problems.' (17-year-old)

There is a downside to growing up

Children and young people are not naive about becoming grown up. Many of them realise that, along with the hoped for possessions and greater freedom, there are some potential disadvantages:

- 'You have to work. There's no choice. You have to get on with your job.' (10-year-old)

- 'You have to do for yourself all the things that your parents did for you before. And, if you go out, you have to pay.' (10-year-old)
- 'You have to take responsibility for what goes wrong – that's part of being grown up.' (12-year-old)
- 'The problem is that you can't mess around any more, or climb up things. You're too big, like at about 20, and people will think you're crazy.' (11-year-old)
- 'You lose the feeling of being young and things you want to do when you're younger. It's still fun playing kids' games, but I don't do it unless I'm with my little cousins.' (13-year-old)
- 'Sometimes when people get older they worry a lot. They bottle it up and it's not easy to talk. They get worried and stressed out, like about getting a good job.' (13-year-old)

A focus on the present

Children and young people may not make direct comparisons between the experience of the generations. They do not have the years of direct personal experience to make the contrast, and lessons on recent history in school are not necessarily applied to people they know. The perspective of young people tends to support an unwillingness to have their parents' experience of previous decades, and sometimes different countries, placed unchanged over their current life.

A number of 13-year-olds summed up their irritation in the following ways:

- 'Sometimes they don't seem to realise that it's the nineties. It's not the same as when they were our age. They say, "When I was young...". But it's not the same now.'
- 'They think that we'll do the same things. My Mum says, "I got married at 18; you'll get married at 18." But I don't want to do that; I want to be a doctor.'
- 'I don't want to hear about the "good old days"! And how all the clothes and the music were better then!'
- 'They get frightened, but then they exaggerate things. The streets were safer in their day, but it's not so bad as they think now.'

Making your own mistakes

Many children and young people recognise, perhaps more than adults sometimes realise, that parents worry about them and wish to protect them. A recurring theme in many individual conversations, and in most of the groups, was that parents cannot push the results of their own experience, and reflection, onto their sons and daughters. The perspective of children and young people is that parents may mean well when they try to offer this short cut to growing up, but that learning cannot work that way.

- 'They want us to learn from their mistakes. But we're not them; we're different people. Sometimes they seem to forget that. We can only learn from our own mistakes.' (13-year-old)
- 'I'm not my Mum. She says, "I had a baby at 16." and she thinks that I will. But I won't; I'm not her.' (13-year-old)
- 'They worry about you getting into trouble. But that shows that they don't trust you. It's important that they trust you.' (11-year-old)
- 'They have to give you a chance. You can't learn unless they let you do things.' (10-year-old)
- 'You can learn by your own mistakes. It's no good adults getting cross. You can't learn unless you make mistakes.' (14-year-old)
- 'Being grown up is taking responsibility for your own mistakes.' (12-year-old)

Conversations with children and young people demonstrate that they take a thoughtful approach to the business of growing up. Their perspective is sometimes different from that of adults, including their parents. Yet young people are aware of much the same range of issues as are adults. Children and young people are often more alert to adults' concerns than adults give them credit for and are prepared to discuss the issues, so long as their views are not overridden by adult opinions.

2. Development from childhood towards adulthood

Individual differences

Studies of children passing from eight years to young adulthood show far too much variation between individuals to allow firm generalisations about '12-year-olds' or absolute predictions of 'by the time they are 15'. It is potentially misleading to give firm ages for many of the changes and evolving abilities that can be seen in girls and boys. The variation also prevents neat descriptions by absolute steps or stages. (The few examples of age in years given in Part two of this book have to be taken only as guidelines.)

Development has to unfold within individual lives. As well as the individuality of each child or young person, there will also be the influence of the social setting in which they live, the ethnic group and culture to which they belong, the impact of whether they are a boy or girl, and their pattern of abilities and disabilities.

This book describes the likely changes as children move into and through the years of adolescence. Yet all of the changes need to be focused within the understanding that children and young people are learning all the time. They are not always learning exactly what adults feel they should learn, and they often reach different conclusions from adults on the basis of very similar information.

Interaction with others

Children and young people do not, of course, develop in isolation. Every day they are in contact with others – children and adults – and are reacting to what they experience. Other people are affected, in turn, by them. Parents have already had to adjust to many changes in their children since babyhood. They continue to experience the impact of more changes as their sons and daughters pass through late childhood and towards adulthood.

Neither children, their families, nor any other setting such as school, are static. All are changing, sometimes more obviously than at other times. Each influences the other through people's behaviour. In the family, changes in children as they develop affect other family members. But, equally, changes in the family – for instance minor or more serious crises – affect children and the way in which they continue to develop further. Sometimes children and young people can be very active in exerting an influence on their setting.

Children with disabilities

The most common source of disability during childhood is the range of different learning disabilities. Physical and sensory disabilities are less frequent overall. Some children are significantly affected by a medical conditions, for instance, cystic fibrosis or cardiac problems.

The development of children and young people is likely to be affected in some way by the impact of disability. However, their opportunities for learning can also be shaped by daily experience, including the extent to which home and school are organised to enable them to learn.

Children with a physical disability may encounter difficulties of moving about or frustrations with play and school materials that are not suitable for their abilities. However, their intellectual and social development may be unfolding in a very similar way to others of their own age. Children with learning disabilities may not be experiencing any frustrations over physical abilities; yet, their social and communication skills may be far more like those of a much younger child. Children with sensory disabilities, for instance in hearing or vision, may need to learn a range of compensatory skills, such as Braille or sign language. They may be more limited in the range of activities, compared with children of a similar age, but part of this impact can be due to expectations in society that everyone can see or hear clearly.

Change and transition

The years of childhood are better seen as a series of changes, as transitions to different ways of handling situations or making sense of the world. The move from child to young adult is not one giant leap, nor a step across the divide on a given birthday. It is a series of steps, some minor, some major and some more easily experienced than others. Adolescence is better viewed as a transitional process, as a steady moving from one state, childhood, into another, adulthood. Many of the issues faced and problems that have to be resolved emerge from this passage, which takes place over a protracted period of time for young people in societies like that of Britain.

The early years of childhood are important but what happens then does not fix children for ever. The positive effects of very happy early years may be chipped away by serious distress in middle childhood. Just as much, children whose early experiences have shaken their trust and affected their learning may recover with positive later experiences.

The 'teenage years'

There is a general myth that children and parents have a quiet time between the beginning of formal school and the inevitable onset of the terrors of the teenage years. This view does not survive either informal conversation with parents and children or consideration of research studies.

Children in the years of middle childhood – roughly the primary school years in Britain – continue to develop. They are learning, and not just within the educational process of school, and they are coping with a wide range of everyday problems and adjustments. The teenage years, usually assumed to be from around 13 years to 17 or 18 years of age, are not always times of appalling upheaval and family conflict. The true situation is far more varied.

Viewpoint

Parents who do not experience the mythic awful time with their young people tend to feel a mixture of puzzlement and good luck. Many parents, whose sons and daughters were on the brink of adulthood have explained, in conversation with the author, how they kept on expecting that some serious crisis must happen.

There seems to be an element of good and bad fortune that blends with parents doing their best. However, many of these parents seemed, to the author, to be less on the receiving end of random luck, than reaping the benefit of offering their young people patience and consideration. Several parents said, 'We had the usual minor disagreements.' but they had weathered these and resisted the temptation to make mountains out of molehills.

A lifespan perspective

One approach to development takes the perspective of the whole life span of individuals. Such a focus moves away from viewing childhood or adolescence as the only times of major change. Adult life has its own, normal crises – some major and some less disruptive. All adults experience, at some time, changes that force adjustment as the transition unfolds. These can be changes such as new partners and marriage, the onset of parenthood, the loss of one's own parents, or changes and disruption in employment. Couples with children have to adjust, one way or another, to changes as their children grow up over the years.

During these kinds of changes and upheavals, adults often find that others – family or friends – can be a source of help and support. Positive relationships between the generations can be very important if young people are to make a psychologically healthy transition to adult-

hood. However, the strength of good friendships can be equally important, and young people are likely to seek different kinds of support
from friends and family.

Making sense of individual differences

Looking carefully at research

The material within this book is drawn from research studies, surveys,
and personal accounts of childhood and adolescence. It is necessary to
be cautious in generalising from the viewpoint of a few children or
young people. Yet, well-established theory, or studies, of childhood or
adolescence can be loaded with the biases of those who undertook the
thinking or research.

Social scientists may be judged, perhaps with hindsight, as strongly
influenced by the values of their own culture, sex or social group. Some
work on childhood and adolescence – for example, some approaches to
moral development – has taken the more traditional, male Western
view as a benchmark and assumed that it applies equally to females.
More recent work has often balanced up this bias and offered alternative perspectives to some theoretical models, models in which particular values seem to have swamped objectivity and respect for varying
values.

Study of the development away from the dependence of childhood
has sometimes taken a view of mature behaviour as an almost total
independence from family. Some cultural traditions foster more of a
sense of interdependence and acceptance of different responsibilities
with the passing years. This is an equally valid approach to this aspect
to growing up, but may not be understood by researchers with a different set of cultural values.

The information that emerges from careful research and the development of theory can contribute to perspectives on children and young
people and sometimes to practical decisions over what course of action
may be for the best. Yet, very frequently, this contribution has to be
couched in terms of 'this looks more likely', 'this is one pattern' and 'it
all depends...' rather than 'this is the answer'.

Sex differences

Discussion of possible differences between the sexes becomes difficult
because the interpretation of any differences is often weighted. It is
rare to hear a conversation in which adults claim a consistent difference between boys and girls, or women and men, and then go on to
suggest that such variety is a positive source of strength for their
society or local community. It is much more frequent that the difference is held as proof that one sex is inherently better than the other.
Consequently, almost any discussion of differences can become both
complicated and emotionally heated. (This is a controversial topic and

readers who would like to follow up the issues will find helpful summaries in Bee, 1994.)

Such differences that are reliably found to be valid will be discussed in the relevant sections of the book. However, there are some key points about making sense of any differences and it is better to address these before any of the description.

Biology or social learning?

Girls and boys clearly are different in one crucial way – girls will grow up to be women and boys to be men. There is a sex difference, that is determined at conception. Males and females are biologically and physiologically different in a number of ways. Two questions then follow:

1. Are there any other areas of development, such as intellectual abilities or communication, in which the sexes are consistently different?
2. To what extent is any variation the result of the sex difference alone?

The answer to the first question is that extensive research has come up with few differences that are consistently found between groups of boys and groups of girls. There is a tremendous amount of variation within both the sexes and, in this way, boys and girls are much more like each other in development and abilities than unlike. The exception is their very different pattern of physical development at puberty. The few remaining areas of consistent difference have to be interpreted with care. The general issues are covered in this section and the more specific in the discussion of areas of development.

The answer to the second question is that it seems most likely that the relatively small differences found between groups of boys and girls are shaped by some combination of biology and social factors. Some of the variation, and for some of the differences perhaps a large part of the explanation, is the consequence of adults' conviction that boys and girls are, or should be, different in specific ways. This conviction leads the adults to behave differently towards children, depending on their sex, and to direct or limit their opportunities.

The available research does not provide the type of information that allows anyone to claim that it is absolutely biology or exclusively social factors that explain the few differences. Nor are there reliable data to assign exact percentages about how much of any difference can be laid at the door of one factor rather than another.

What might the differences mean?

There are four crucial points about the research data on female–male differences. These have to be remembered in any discussion of sex differences:

1. *The differences are averages and not absolute*
   These are average differences, reached by testing many children and young people. On most of the differences described, there is a great deal of overlap between the boys and girls.
   So, within each sex there is almost the full possible range of abilities or types of behaviour. One of the few exceptions is the data that indicate boys are more likely than girls to show almost all of the kinds of physical, emotional and intellectual vulnerability to stress (see pages 62 and 71).

2. *Some differences have been found, but are usually very small*
   Even when the differences are very clear, as is the case with the greater aggressiveness of males over females, the average differences are still small.

3. *There is no basis for making simple predictions from group data to individuals*
   There is still a great deal of individual variation that is not explained or predicted by sex. For instance, the statistical fact that groups of adolescent boys have, so far, typically produced better average scores on mathematical reasoning than groups of adolescent girls does not predict that any individual boy will score highly, nor that any individual girl will produce a low score. Nor do these data predict that this difference will necessary hold true for future generations.

4. *Different does not equal better*
   There is nothing in the research that justifies any claim that the small differences prove that one sex is better than another. Many of the problems in discussing possible sex differences come from the rush to heavily subjective interpretation.

In Britain, although society has changed a great deal, the balance of interpretation still tends, frequently, to favour males over females. In acknowledgement of this bias one may have to stress that the data indicating girls' better, on average, articulation and verbal reasoning do not go to show that females talk too much. Boys' greater average aggressiveness cannot be inevitably taken as a positive trait of leadership and a case needs to be made to question why this pattern is so often dismissed during discussions when it is claimed that it is females who are too 'emotional'.

The nature of development

The blend between different aspects of development

Part two describes many of the changes that happen as children develop towards young adulthood. These changes are organised into different kinds of development, since otherwise the description would become very unwieldy. However, boys and girls do not experience separate 'tunnels' of development, for instance, for physical or intellectual aspects. What is happening to children and young people in one part of development, and the sense that they make of it, will usually be affecting other aspects as well.

Using abilities

Anyone involved with young children – parents or professional early years workers – soon recognises the linked issues of the question, 'Is it that she can't do it, or more that she doesn't want to?' During late childhood and adolescence, the issue of active choice becomes even more important. For example, a ten-year-old girl may be very capable of holding a lively conversation and expressing carefully considered opinions. However, in certain circumstances, she chooses to give one-word answers and appears taciturn and uncommunicative. Perhaps a 14-year-old boy has plenty of talent in scientific matters, but chooses to play around in class and so misses vital opportunities to understand the subject.

There will always be reasons for the choices of children and young people. The ten-year-old girl may feel less confident with unfamiliar adults, or may be judging, perhaps correctly, that a given adult is not genuinely interested in what she has to say. The 14-year-old boy may be weighing up his sense of obligation to parents and teachers against the more pressing – for the moment – attraction of fitting in with his friends and the short-term kudos of baiting the science teacher. Such conflicting pressures can sometimes emerge through a calm conversation with an adult, especially if that adult suppresses his or her conviction that the reasons are just 'not good enough!'. The difficulty for caring and involved adults is in controlling their own sense of frustration over wasted opportunities.

Perhaps one of the forgotten aspects of the development of older children and young people is their growing awareness of how much more they have to learn. They can be enthusiastic and excited about this continuing prospect, although some are wary about how much more is to come. But what can also happen is that an acceptance of higher standards in all areas undermines their confidence about existing abilities. The quotation in the box sums it up well. The role of adults, parents and teachers can be to support children so that they do not lose so much of their sense of excitement and wonder as the responsibilities of later childhood rest heavily upon them.

'Ask a kindergarten class, "How many of you can draw?" and all hands shoot up. Yes, of course we can draw – all of us. What can you draw? Anything! How about a dog eating a fire truck in a jungle! Sure! How big do you want it?

How many of you can sing? All hands. Of course we sing! What can you sing? Anything! What if you don't know the words? No problem, we make them up....

Their answer is Yes! Over and over again, Yes! The children are confident in spirit, infinite in resources, and eager to learn. Everything is still possible.

Try those same questions on a college audience. A small percentage of the students will raise their hands when asked if they draw or dance or sing or paint or act or play an instrument. Not infrequently, those who do raise their hands will want to qualify their response with their limitations: "I only play piano, I only draw horses, I only dance to rock and roll, I only sing in the shower."

When asked why the limitations, college students answer that they do not have talent, are not majoring in the subject ... or that they are too embarrassed for others to see them sing or dance. ...

What went wrong between kindergarten and college?

What happened to YES! of course I can?'

From Robert Fulghum (1991) *Uh-oh – some observations from both sides of the refridgerator door*. Ivy Books: New York

Part two: Development of children and young people

3. Physical development

Physical skills and games

The development of very young children is full of the highly visible milestones, such as learning to crawl, to walk and to run about. By the time that children have reached their eighth birthday, the majority of them will have a range of basic physical skills. Individual children apply their skills in different ways, depending on the opportunities they are offered and the choices that they make.

Children who have physical disabilities may well have limits on the kind of activities that are possible, or feasible without supporting equipment. Some children will have continuing health conditions that may circumscribe their possibilities in exercise, or mean that they, or a responsible adult, have to monitor their level of exercise, for their own well-being.

The range of possibilities

Physical play

Children of eight years and older use their physical skills in spontaneous games of their own devising – running, chasing and climbing. In open spaces or on the pavements some children show how skilled they have become in controlling a bike, or in achieving balance with equipment such as roller skates or in-line blades.

More organised games

Children now have good control of hand or foot and can coordinate their movement with what they see. Younger children can handle some equipment but older girls and boys are far more able to control a small cricket or rounders bat and to connect with a small or large ball. Children's physical skills combine with their greater social skills and this development means that organised games, with rules, are far more possible than tends to be the case with younger children. Children play football in informal groups as well as in games organised by schools. Depending on what is on offer, they are also capable of learning the specific skills of cricket, rounders, tennis, netball, rugby and many other team games.

New physical skills

Children can become adept at swimming and diving, at horse riding or ice skating. They can enjoy and improve their skill in activities such as different forms of dance, judo or karate. But these and similar skills are very unlikely to be learned unless children have access to the relevant facilities, and adults who will coach them – not necessarily formally.

A great deal will depend on the opportunities available, either locally or through organised trips. For instance, it has become increasingly common for schools to offer older children and young people the opportunity of going on physical adventure days or residential holidays. In well run and safe facilities it can become obvious just how much potential rests within the eight to 18 years age range. Such trips are the only way that most children will be able to gain the skills of controlling small boats, climbing or abseiling.

Boys' and girls' games

By eight years of age, children can be very aware that some games are generally regarded as more for one sex than the other. Schools, after-school and holiday schemes, and some families, may try hard to work against this view. However, there are still enough adults who take the view that some games are more appropriate for one sex than the other. Hence, some children and young people will bring these views to their play and organised games.

The strength of adults who want a more equal approach to games playing is that they can create the opportunities for mixed-sex games. They may also have given children enough confidence to deal with the potential difficulties of stepping across a gender barrier.

Viewpoint

Two twelve-year-old girls described how they had dealt with the boys in the cricket coaching sessions they attended:

'In the first few sessions the boys were down on us. If one of us made a mistake, then it was, "Huh, girls!" If we did a good shot, then it was, "Lucky!" We didn't rise to it; we just kept playing, and we'd say, "Well done!" for their good shots, and "Bad luck!" for some of their mistakes. And then they slowly came round, and treated us like we were treating them – and like they were treating each other.'

The increase in popularity of different kinds of exercise class seems to have given young women further options for keeping fit, especially for those who are not attracted to team games.

Physical activity and health

Regular exercise during the years of childhood supports long-term health, because early habits can establish a physically active lifestyle. So, it is important that children and young people find physical pursuits, from the range available, that they enjoy playing and are motivated later to organise themselves to continue.

For many children and young people the direction and extent of the development of their physical skills will depend on the following factors:

- Having somewhere safe to play physical games.
- The availability of basic equipment that works reasonably well and is in a fair condition. Brand new equipment is attractive, but many children and young people would happily settle for something that just does the job.
- Support and encouragement of children as they learn the techniques and pass through the inevitable stage in learning any physical skill when the moves and coordinations are far from automatic.
- Access to facilities for sports and physical activities. Parents are often the ones who have to provide the transport to get children to centres when no realistic public transport is available or the journey would mean walking alone in the dark.

- An enjoyable experience of physical activity. Children vary in level of skill and one child may always be a more talented footballer or tennis player, no matter how hard her friend practises. So, a great deal can depend on how children are encouraged and supported in enjoying their own level of skill.
- Children and young people need a balance between physical and other pursuits. Also, they may not wish to pursue the same activities throughout childhood and early adulthood.

The role of adults

Children and young people benefit from the encouragement of adults – parents, teachers and coaches in physical pursuits. But, there are probably limits to how far a child's interest should become an adult's absorption. It can be tempting for adults to believe that developing talent or even a child's mild interest in a physical activity should be taken with immense seriousness. Children may well share this conviction for some time and then commitment to, for instance, swimming club begins to impinge on other activities – study or social – that they wish to pursue. Adults who coach individuals or teams have to accept that even talented young people will have other interests and obligations. They may not wish to give up other activities to the extent that will be required for a real dedication to excellence.

Parents are welcome at games and on the touchline, so long as they realise that their child is the focus. Parents whose self-esteem has become bound in their children's or the team's success can become an embarrassment to their sons and daughters. In extreme cases, parents have been banned from games by frustrated referees.

Attitudes towards physical activities

There has been concern expressed by health care professionals that children and young people are less physically active than previous generations. There seem to be several possible reasons for this:

- Parents' concerns over their children's safety has led to less independent travel, such as walking and cycling to school or to leisure activities. It is also possible that they allow them out onto the streets and parks less, or not until an older age, compared with previous generations. (More on page 117.)
- Children and young people often have the attractions of more sedentary pursuits, such as watching television or video and playing computer games.
- There has been a decline in physical education lessons and extra-curricular activities in schools, which may be some young people's main opportunity for physical activity. For instance, in 1990 71 per cent of under-14s in state schools had less than two hours of PE a week. There are some indications that this trend is now reversing.

- Currently, estimates are that 11- to 16-year-old boys are twice as likely to take active physical exercise than girls, although it is looking as if this gap may close somewhat. The explanation may be one of opportunities. However, it seems just as likely that the girls are regarding physically energetic activities as inappropriate for them once they are becoming young women.

For individual children, the explanations probably involve some combination of reasons.

Physical disabilities

Some older children and young people will be experiencing the continued impact of physical disabilities that were present at birth or which developed in early childhood. Children become increasingly aware of what their friends and peers can manage and they may be very conscious of the gap created by their disability.

A great deal will depend on the severity of a child's physical disability but also on the practical help and emotional support that is available. Specially adapted equipment is an undoubted help, but the value may be lessened if adult support does not ensure that children with disabilities are enabled to join in as much of the physical activity as possible. Other children can, of course, be impatient or cruel about disabilities, but are not inevitably so. Adults have a responsibility to take the consistent approach that everyone has a pattern of greater or lesser ability in the different physical possibilities.

For some children or young people, the experience of disability comes suddenly, as the consequence of accidental injury. They are then coming to terms with a serious emotional adjustment to the temporary, or more permanent, change in their life, as well as the physical results of injury.

Young people whose injuries require them to use wheelchairs probably take several years to adjust fully to their changed mobility. Everyday tasks and what were formerly normal activities are very likely to take longer, if they are done without assistance. The young people discover personally the many restrictions to easy access for wheelchair users.

Fine physical skills

Children are also honing their abilities within art, craft and design. Much as with the more energetic physical activities, children's potential to extend their skills and interest will depend on what is available to them. Some children are offered a wider range of activities, or have the advantage of greater encouragement from adults.

Art and craft activities

Children and young people can enjoy a wide array of craft activities and different kinds of artwork. Some individuals will show a striking talent in design or execution of a project in particular skill areas. Talented children deserve encouragement and challenging projects. However, all children can gain satisfaction and enjoyment whatever their level of skill.

Older children have the coordination to manage materials and tools and greater patience to see through more complex projects. Children and young people can use their skills on small scale crafts and larger scale building projects, for instance, in adventure playgrounds.

They are increasingly capable of organising their choice of materials and colours, and designing what they wish to make. Their physical skills are working together with their increased ability to look ahead and consider what they want or need to make.

Children will vary in which activities they find most absorbing, and part of this difference may be the enthusiasm and coaching abilities of the adults who introduce them to a skill. Children also tend to feel more involved with an end product that promises to be useful, exciting or impressive.

Daily life

Children and young people also show their growing abilities if they are given a role within the domestic arena of family life. They are very capable of learning cooking skills, gardening or helping out in a safe way with general maintenance or mending. This kind of encouragement of physical skills does not have to be a burden – in fact, children are often pleased to have their skills and sense of responsibility recognised.

4. The changes of puberty

The onset of puberty is a major physical and emotional adjustment for older children and young people.

The beginning of puberty

There is a wide age range for the start and completion of all the changes that make up puberty. For instance, some girls of ten may have started their periods and are already wearing a bra. Since the start of menstruation is relatively late in the whole sequence for girls, the ten-year-old who has her periods will have started the whole process a couple of years earlier. Other girls will not be at her stage until closer to 14 years old.

On average – that constant reminder about any discussion of sex differences – girls are maturing faster and earlier than boys. This difference is especially noticeable in the development before birth and then during puberty. Boys are starting puberty at around ten years old at the earliest and some may be as late as 16 years.

There are both visible and less obvious changes within the sequence of puberty and the whole process takes some time. The changes that will move an individual from child to the beginnings of a young adult start in the brain. Messages are sent from the hypothalamus to the pituitary gland. This gland then releases hormones which enlarge the testes in boys and the ovaries in girls. The testes then manufacture the sex hormone testosterone and the ovaries make oestrogen. These sex hormones start the other physical changes of puberty.

Children are often aware of the changes that are to come. They may have noticed older brothers and sisters or been observant generally. Some have had a number of conversations with their parents, or gained knowledge during primary school sex education lessons. Some children worry about what puberty will be like for them; others appear to ignore the entire prospect until it has obviously started.

The main changes

The experience of puberty is different for boys and girls since the whole process is moving them into adulthood for their own sex.

Differences between the sexes

The first clear physical signs of puberty for boys are an increase in the rate of growth of their testes and scrotum, followed by the development of pubic hair. Their penis also enlarges towards its final adult size. Boys experience erections and start to produce seminal fluid. Daytime erections are not necessarily linked with sexual thoughts, and there may be no ejaculation. Nightime erections may well be followed by ejaculation – the so-called 'wet dream'.

Viewpoint

Young people in individual conversations sometimes express relief that parents, or sometimes older brothers and sisters, passed on experiences that were more than factual information.

One 14-year-old boy mentioned a helpful conversation with his father: 'Dad said to me about how your penis seems to have a life of its own. How you get erections for no good reason; he called them "test runs". He said that it used to happen to him in maths lessons. I'm glad he told me; I'd have wondered what was going on. And it was a maths lesson!'

For girls, growth of their breasts and the first signs of pubic hair are the earliest visible signs. The start of periods comes relatively late in the whole sequence for girls. There are internal changes for girls in that their ovaries, uterus, fallopian tubes and vagina are all increasing in size.

Shared experiences

Girls and boys develop the secondary sexual characteristics of body hair – the pubic and underarm hair, but also additional hair on arms and legs. Boys are usually more hairy overall than girls and develop the male facial hair. The extent of hair growth is variable and individual differences seem to be genetic.

The decision over hair removal is a cultural tradition, for both sexes. Some cultures leave males with an individual decision about whether to grow a moustache and beard, or to be clean shaven. Whereas other cultures, sometimes for religious reasons, value the growth of a beard as an important symbol of being an adult male. This tradition can lead to potential conflict in schools where it is not usual to tolerate facial hair for the older male pupils.

It is equally the case that hair removal for females, for instance on legs or under arms, is also a cultural tradition that varies around the world. The prevailing view in Britain encourages removal, with the firm implication that body hair is unfeminine.

The related changes in the bodies of boys and girls bring about a change towards a more adult body odour and the need for closer atten-

tion to personal hygiene, especially after physical exercise. Some of the hormonal changes can give young people skin problems that they previously did not have. Many young people have problems with spots – varying from mild to extensive – and some have more persistent and troublesome acne.

Both sexes experience a deepening in their voice, although the change is usually more obvious with boys. Some boys also experience sudden changes in the pitch of their voice.

The growth spurt

Overall size

Girls tend to have their growth spurt earlier on in the entire process than boys. Since girls, on average, start puberty earlier than boys this leads to a situation in which some girls find themselves taller than boys of their age, until the boys start to grow at a fast pace.

In both girls and boys, the sex hormones work together with the growth hormones, also produced by the pituitary gland, and these trigger the growth spurt of height and weight. For boys, this often dramatic change can happen as early as ten years old or as late as 16 years. For girls, the onset may be as young as nine or ten years, or as late as 13 or 14 years. Looking at averages, the most rapid growth period for boys tends to be at 13 to 14 years and for girls at 11 to 13 years. Overall girls' physical growth tends to be more regular and predictable, whereas boys are more likely to experience the visibly uneven growth spurts.

When boys and girls are in the growth spurt they grow swiftly, leaving clothes and shoe sizes in their wake. Girls can grow as much as 100 mm in one year, boys as much as 120 mm. The growth of young people is not restricted to adding height and weight. Their internal organs are also growing. There is a parallel growth in the functioning of the heart and lungs and the size and strength of many of the muscles in the body. Both sexes find a marked increase in physical strength and endurance.

Strength

There is little consistent difference between boys and girls in strength and speed until the changes brought about by puberty. Then boys start to become stronger and faster than girls – on average.

A practical issue can arise within mixed sex play and the boy–girl friendships that survive the teasing of middle childhood. Girls who used to be able to hold their own physically with male playmates begin to find that their companions can hurt or wind them. This is probably without intention, since the boys literally do not know their own growing strength.

Body shape and weight

Both girls and boys are changing in overall body shape. Body weight can even double between ten to 18 years. Part of this is explained by increased height but young people also become bulkier. For boys, the additional weight has a much larger proportion of muscle to fat than is the case for girls. The girls develop muscle, but they also put on fat, around the hips, breasts and shoulders, which leads to a more rounded, adult female shape. Young men within this stage still tend to be slighter than adult males and continue to broaden, perhaps until their mid-twenties.

Possible concerns about puberty

Timing

Girls and boys have to accept the sequence that unfolds for them in puberty. There may be a genetic basis to whether a child will be an early, average or a late developer. Poor nutrition can be a delaying factor, as can excessive physical exercise for girls, for instance, very strict training programmes in gymnastics or running.

Studies of individuals in puberty suggest that, for boys, being an early developer is, by and large, an advantage during those years that they look more grown up than their peers. Boys who are noticeably late in the onset of puberty seem more likely to have problems of an emotional nature, as they worry about being left behind in height, weight and other characteristics of adult maleness. Neither the advantage of early, nor the worries of late puberty seem necessarily to persist into later years.

For girls, early maturation seems to be a mixed experience. Girls may feel confident to look more grown up. Alternatively, some feel ill at ease with their new body, in contrast with friends who are more childlike. Parents also worry about a daughter who looks considerably older than her actual years. Practical issues arise for girls who start periods during the primary years, since some schools are not properly equipped for disposal of sanitary products. On the other hand, noticeably late development can lead girls to worry, with them experiencing a sense of lagging behind their friends and acquaintances. They may also be treated by adults as more like a child than a young person.

It is probably inevitable that children and young people compare themselves with others as they pass through puberty and that this happens whatever their rate of development. Girls and boys look towards their peers and sometimes this comparison may lead them to feel happy with themselves. At other times, both sexes may feel inadequate over their height, general shape or skin eruptions.

Viewpoint

Young people going through puberty do not all fret all the time, but many are very conscious of what is happening and is yet to come.

As one 12-year old girl expressed it:

'I'll be pleased when puberty is over and done with. There are so many worries about spots and breasts and periods. Everyone I know thinks that some part of their body is fat. You feel really self-conscious. Little pimples that you think everyone can see, and you make it worse because you're fiddling with it so much. You can't wake up without something else being on your mind – whether it's friends, your body or something.'

Any comparisons can also be jarring within the family. Brothers and sisters can be a great support to each other but, on the other hand, they can be a source of relentless teasing. Younger children in the family may become concerned if their personal timetable for puberty seems to be later than their older brother or sister, whom they watched some years previously. Puberty can also be a testing time for twins. There is no reason why non-identical twins should go through puberty in tandem and, in a boy-girl pair, the girl may well start earlier than her brother. Pre-birth factors may even lead to a discrepancy for identical twins.

Taking medical advice

There is a great deal of variation between individuals in the onset and pattern of puberty. However, a very early or very delayed onset would be good reason for parents and young people to consult the family doctor. A possible start to further reading on this issue is Smith and Fenwick, 1993.

Adjustment to changing shape

There is often a certain unevenness in the growth spurt which can make girls and boys feel ungainly. Arms and legs seem to be over long and out of proportion to the rest of their body, and a temporary feeling of clumsiness can result. It often happens that young people reach their final shoe size before they have completed the rest of their growth and they spend some time – probably less than they believe – with feet that feel too big for the rest of them.

Girls and young women passing through puberty start to feel fatter because they are fatter. They are a different shape – not necessarily overweight. Female attitudes to changing shape depend a great deal on the messages that they are receiving about standards of attractiveness. If their social and cultural group values a naturally rounded female shape and celebrates this as part of growing up, then young women are more likely to welcome the changes. Where the admired female figures are almost pre-pubescent, then most young women will either fail in their vision of attractiveness or follow stringent, possibly unhealthy, patterns of dieting.

Viewpoint

It can help if parents remember with honesty their own experience of puberty. Their children's experience will not be the same – partly because they are different individuals and partly because the pressures on this generation are slightly different. But, a sensitive understanding of the feelings may support a sympathetic approach.

One mother contrasted her experience with that of her daughter.

'I was a teenager in the sixties and all of us girls were obsessed about our bust measurement. We all nagged our mothers to let us buy padded bras. Now, my daughter and her friends want to be like these 5ft 7in, seven and a half stone models. And they can't do it without dieting. It worries me and makes me angry at the same time. Not with the girls themselves – but with the stupid pressures on them from outside.'

Boys can also be concerned about their size and shape. Some may be concerned to lose weight, although this seems to be the boys and young men who are actually overweight. Others are concerned to fill out and have the kind of muscle and tone that does not simply appear overnight, but needs specific physical exercise to achieve.

Offering help and support

Children and young people talk about the events of puberty among themselves, just as they discuss many issues in their lives. Girls and boys may offer friends support over this time and can be a source of reliable information. Unfortunately, peers – even friends – can delight in being rude about a boy or girl's relative stage of development.

It is important that adults should explain to children the kind of changes that will come to boys and girls. Without prior knowledge, children can be surprised or distressed by what are perfectly natural events, taking them towards adulthood. The information passed by word of mouth between children and young people is not always reliable, and can be drastically wrong on occasions. Parents and teachers can be equally important in offering support because they hold different roles.

Children with learning disabilities need just as much support from parents in order to understand the changes and to move steadily towards a more mature approach, within their capabilities. Parents of children with severe learning disabilities can be very concerned about the kind of adult life that will be feasible for their son or daughter (see also page 112).

The school curriculum

A well planned sex education programme in primary school, or at the latest in early secondary, can communicate information through various media – books and booklets, videos and invited speakers. The other potential advantage is the opportunity for guided group discussion.

Obviously the quality of a discussion will be very dependent on the person who leads it – whether this is a teacher or someone else. When discussion works well, children and young people appreciate the chance to talk about the issues involved in puberty, the sexual element in relationships, and babies. They will probably not want to ask very personal questions in an open group, but many of them want to talk around the topic. In a coeducational school, there can be good reasons to have some single-sex discussions, but older children and young people often express a wish to have at least some mixed-sex groups, since they want to hear 'the other side'.

Parents have the right to withdraw their children from the separate sex education lessons within the National Curriculum. However, no withdrawal is allowed from the sex education part of the science curriculum.

> **Viewpoint**
>
> In the early 1990s newspapers reported, with some relish, complaints about the questions that some older children had asked in sex education classes. The issue became sensationalised and some commentators appeared to be very naive about the conversations that regularly go on in playgrounds. Children do not have to look far to become aware of a range of adult sexual practices. In fact, all they have to do is to read a newspaper regularly! They may not understand what they read and, in those circumstances, they ask a question.
>
> Experienced teachers are very capable of fielding both the questions that are a genuine wish for information and the wind-ups. They are also, as several teachers told the author, very capable of suggesting to a pupil, "This is a question that you should really ask your parents."

Help from home

Children can hear information together and some of them, more probably the girls, may well continue with discussions outside the classroom. Parents are in the best position to deal with questions or worries as they emerge and to talk over the feelings of this time of life, as and when children and young people want to have a conversation.

Conversations

It helps to be ready to talk about what will happen in puberty while children are still some years away from the beginning. If parents are in the habit of having conversations with their children and answering questions honestly, then opportunities will arise. It is unwise for parents to attempt to cover everything in one lengthy sitting, or to assume that handing over a book will do the job completely.

If children do not ask questions, and some do not, then it is sensible to broach the topic sooner rather than later – bearing in mind that some children will be starting puberty while they are still in primary school.

Empathy for children's feelings

Parents, or anyone else in whom children confide, should take children and young people's concerns seriously, while reassuring them when appropriate. Boys and girls may need to be reminded of the wide variation between people, or of the fact that most young people worry at some point about how they look. Parents cannot affect the timing of puberty, but they can be available to listen to their son or daughter's feelings about where they are in the process.

Mothers and fathers need also to remember that puberty takes a lot of young people's energy and concern and that they can be sensitive about what is happening to them. Young people are unlikely to appreciate teasing or public comments, even within the family, about the changes. It is not unusual for young people to want more privacy in the bathroom and in their bedroom.

Parents' own feelings

Parents have adjustments of their own to manage. Perhaps a son or daughter's puberty triggers parents' own memories of growing up. They also have to adjust to the reality that children are no longer 'my little girl or boy'. Boys and girls are awakening to a sense of their own sexuality and their attractiveness may matter a great deal to them. For some this will develop as an attraction to their own sex. There is more on sexuality and partnerships starting on page 144.

5.   The skills of communication

Talking and understanding

Children's ability to communicate and to understand the communication of others is central to much of their development. Most eight-year-olds are confident in one language and some will be fluent in two or more. Children vary in their level of confidence in speaking up and this can be most noticeable when they are in unusual or more formal situations.

Children and young people have the potential to listen and understand what is said to them. Whether they do listen will depend partly on whether they have learned to value listening to others. Some children's experience is that few people listen to them and show respect for their views. If this is the case, the children themselves tend to copy that model. Even good listeners will fade away when they are bored, tired or judge that the speaker is 'going on' unreasonably.

Uses of language

Children and young people continue to increase their working vocabulary as their knowledge extends into different topics. As well as the actual words at their command, eight-year-olds are already capable of a wide use of language. This development can continue through childhood and into adolescence.

Children and young people are capable of using their language skills in many different ways, for instance to:

- express thoughts or to work through an idea out loud;
- put feelings into words;
- argue a case, explain or justify an action;
- describe and recount what has happened;
- question and find out more or to seek an explanation;
- offer support to friends or family, express sympathy;
- exchange opinions on a wide variety of topics and to support their views or argue with others;
- weigh up and come to decisions or judgements on the basis of information;
- challenge or use in a defensive way during an argument or confrontation.

Conversations

Eight-year-olds can hold a confident conversation on a topic that holds their interest. Sometimes adults may be less than impressed with the choice of special interest that children or young people make. Parents, for instance, may not want their sons or daughters to invest computer games with great importance or take television soap operas seriously. Yet adults are likely to get much further by showing some respect for children's choices. If they ask genuine questions and listen properly to the answers, then adults are far more likely to build the basis for conversations on other topics.

Children can learn ground rules for courteous communication with one or more people, but a great deal will depend on the behaviour of adults in introducing such guidance and providing a consistent model to follow. Children and young people will learn the ground rules of their own social and cultural group. Talking together becomes an important part of friendships for children and young people and such conversations appear to follow different patterns for boys and girls (see page 138).

Communication in groups

Children and young people vary in their level of confidence and some are more forthcoming in communication with just one person. However, many learn to speak up as well as listen during the give and take of a small group and also in a larger group, such as a whole class discussion. Children of primary school age can become confident speaking in a more public setting – for instance, by presenting work in school assemblies.

Young people can become adept in debating skills and in putting their case in a persuasive style. Part of this skill is learning to identify the opposing views, and their support, and making an effective counter-answer. As with many skills, some young people will develop particular talents in debating.

To think about

Western European cultures tend to value speaking up in a group, asking questions and even differing in opinion from teachers. Some Oriental cultures, in contrast, do not value this kind of assertiveness and some discourage even mild disagreement with older and more experienced adults. Such behaviour is seen as very discourteous.

Children and young people can often be more able to adapt than adults and grasp that different settings require different communication styles. However, adults in positions such as teacher need to understand that their own cultural tradition, whatever that may be, is not universal.

Awareness of different kinds of language

Children will have become aware of different accents and of different versions of the same language. Young people may well consciously use a different style of speech for varying circumstances – for instance, in talking with friends as opposed to speaking up in class. They can become aware, often with help, that particular styles of conversation are more suitable for specific situations, for instance, attending a job or college interview.

Children, who have not learned a second, or third language within the family, will be capable of extending their skills. British schools

tend to postpone introducing new lang
stage. However, younger children are v
tional language, and are sometimes kee

Disabilities affecting communication

For some children and young people, their di
or possibility of communication. Difficulties of
caused by a number of different reasons.

Blind or partially-sighted children have to u
many instances will limit written communication. I   or
total loss of vision makes unavailable much of the i   about
who is talking and the non-verbal part of any messa   hildren or
young people with severe difficulties in forming words may be understood less well than a child who is deaf. Children with learning disabilities may not have developed sufficient language to be able to speak or
to be understood.

Communication difficulties that arise from hearing loss may be
partly overcome by a hearing aid, but children can experience difficulty when they are in a noisy environment and many conversations
are going on simultaneously. Also, children and young people are
sometimes self-conscious about wearing an aid, or reminding friends
or teachers that they need a clear view of someone's face in order to
lip-read.

The ease of communication will depend on cooperation from others,
their willingness to learn signing, where appropriate, and the availability of useful equipment to support clear communication. For
instance, some pupils with hearing loss may be helped by a hand-held
microphone unit, which they give to each teacher in turn. Some schools
have induction loops which make it possible for children with hearing
difficulties to pick up more frequencies.

Reading and writing

Eight-year-olds should be able to read and write, although some will
be finding this easier or more enjoyable than others. Some eight-year-
olds may be having serious difficulty with the written word and will
not be making noticeable progress. If this is the case, then it is time for
careful assessment of the source of their difficulties and planning of
appropriate help.

Through the years of school, children and young people are potentially able to extend their skills.

Reading widely

Reading and writing both need considerable practice for children to
become confident in using the skills in the many different ways they
offer. With plenty of practice, children become able to read more difficult texts and to retain what they have read. Ideally, children and

young people should be reading a range of material, including books for pleasure. Unfortunately, some young people continue to feel that reading – and writing too – is basically a school chore and not a leisure activity.

Children become adept at expressing an opinion about what they have read. Initially, this may be through conversation, moving on to writing short book reviews. With encouragement, they can express straightforward and then increasingly complex ideas about why a book is 'good' or 'bad'. Within primary school children can be starting to analyse what makes a book or poem work and looking at characterisation in some detail.

Using resources

Older children and young people are capable of becoming much more critical readers and bringing together different written material around a theme. They can track down and assess information. The emphasis in the National Curriculum, for many subjects, is to help young people to evaluate different kinds of written sources and their likely reliability. They compare different accounts of the same event or literary approaches to a similar topic.

Writing skills

Children improve their physical writing skills, so that their work flows more easily. There is a great deal of variation between children, but spelling, punctuation and grammar can improve with good teaching. By the end of primary school children should have a grasp of planning and organising their work and these skills can improve as the years pass.

Children and young people become able to write longer pieces of work but they are also learning about different styles of writing for different kinds of publications and aims. The National Curriculum requires 14- and 15-year-olds to produce written coursework, some of which requires careful research and planning.

Computer skills

Computer literacy

The current generation of children and young people have access to computer technology, both at a level and at an early age that would have seemed unlikely to occur in their parents' childhood, and pure science fiction in their grandparents' youth. Additionally, children and young people will now enter a world of work in which, for many jobs, it will be crucial that they are confident in solving problems and communicating using computers.

Children can gain confidence in working with computers and in using the technology in household equipment such as videos or microwave ovens. Adults need to alert children to appropriate care with and of expensive equipment. However, children's natural propensity to play is an advantage when learning the basic commands in simple programmes or experimenting with different software packages. For instance, eight- and nine-year-olds may be happily creating pictures with a 'draw' package long before they need to use this skill to make an accurate, more technical drawing.

Children are now expected to become confident with computers during the primary school years. They are not just learning particular packages but are also using the capabilities of computer technology to learn and to produce their work. By the end of primary school, children will be expected to manage the following at a basic level:

- Make some sensible choices between different kinds of software, in order to do different jobs in a project. For example, is this a piece of writing or is it a drawing or an item of information for the database?
- Use the computer to organise and type up their own work.
- Get into and move around a simple database – adding and finding information in the files.
- Make some progress when faced with a new machine, because they have learned what sort of commands should be available and the basic structure of files.

A great deal depends on the equipment that is available to children and some are undoubtedly struggling on aging and temperamental systems, or waiting in a queue for their turn.

Parents will, of course, vary in their own confidence and skill with computers. Depending on age and experience, some parents may find that their children and young people are considerably more comfortable with a computer than they are. Schools should provide computers for use in the classroom. Families may not be able to afford to buy their own computer, however, if this is feasible option then it is wise to buy a system that will allow a good range of software packages and not one limited to mainly games.

Using the Internet

Some families with home computers decide to link up to the Internet. Parents who work from home may be linked up for business reasons. Access to the Internet offers a breathtakingly large amount of information that can be reached, once users have worked out how to move about on the 'information highway'. It is possible to communicate with other users via the screen and to join the myriad of discussion groups.

There has been increasing concern that children and young people could gain access to unsuitable material, especially that of a pornographic nature. Undoubtedly there are some visual images and written exchanges on the Internet that should seriously concern parents.

However, such material is a small proportion of the total information available.

Access is not through a simple command on the screen as soon as the link is made to the Internet. It takes deliberate effort and special programmes are required to convert coded material into pictures and sound. However, young people who are experienced with computers and motivated can find the material, especially if they are permitted by parents to spend considerable time without supervision.

Commercial providers, such as Compuserve, who facilitate the link to the Internet, keep a watch on content. Software is also being developed that can restrict access to particular areas. However, concerned parents need to monitor their children's total time on line as well as taking an active interest in what they choose to access. Similar guidelines apply to the monitoring of Internet use as apply to children's use of computer games. Additionally, close scrutiny of telephone bills will show whether sons or daughters are spending excessive amounts of time on line, since access operates through a telephone line.

Computer games

The related expansion affecting children's lives has been the veritable explosion of home computer games. Strictly speaking not all are 'computer' games, since some systems work through a television set and some games are hand-held systems.

Adults worry that children and young people will become compulsive about playing computer games and that it may swamp their homework or other leisure activities. Headlines about 'computer junkies' may sell papers but they do not seem to be an accurate reflection of what goes on in most homes. Additionally, the majority of the research undertaken so far has been on arcade games, when the concern is not only about the nature of the game but the social environment of the arcade.

The key points that arise are as follows:

- Excessive time spent on any one activity is probably unwise. For instance, physical activity is beneficial for health, but four or five hours every day in the gym would not be recommended.
- Long periods of repetitive movement can have painful physical consequences, which is the reason why adults who work at a computer screen are advised to take a break every hour or so.
- The question arises of what children or young people are not doing as a consequence of long hours of game playing. Are they failing to get much fresh air, or enjoy some vigorous physical activity? Are they playing games rather than talking with friends and family or completing obligations such as homework? Exactly the same questions should also be asked about long hours of television viewing.
- Another approach is to consider what the games players may be gaining from the activity. The answer depends somewhat on the

games being played. Most will give practice with quick reactions, active recall of the consequences of previous routes taken, assessment of strategies and some kinds of problem solving. Some games, for example Sym City or Myst, require some exacting decisions and weighing up of possible actions.

Computer games, like television and video viewing, are an area of leisure activity in which parents need to be ready to intervene and offer alternatives, but without the broad assumption that the activity is nothing but a waste of time.

6. Intellectual development

Within the years of late childhood and adolescence, boys and girls are extending their knowledge of facts and the framework in which to make sense of further information. They are also growing in their ability to think and to apply the results of careful thought. They are extending their powers of logic and reasoning. A considerable amount of this kind of learning happens within their educational experience, but it is not restricted to within the boundaries of school. None of the changes happen overnight and in many cases children show adults that they have shifted to a different level of thinking, rather than experienced a dramatic change in everything.

The growth of knowledge

By eight years of age children have already amassed a great deal of information. There are many gaps in their understanding and some misunderstandings that will not be cleared up until later. From eight to 18 years there is great potential for children and young people to extend their knowledge tremendously, but this development involves more than simply adding on a large quantity of facts.

In school, new areas of knowledge continue to be introduced and different skills are required. So children and young people are in a position of having to tolerate, on a regular basis, not knowing about a subject or being at the stage of coming to grips with new information or techniques. With good support, both children and young people can regard this experience as more of a challenge and opportunity than a threat. However, many adults probably underestimate the stress that not knowing or not yet understanding can place on children, even confident children. Children or young people can become very uneasy, or even give up, if they continue to feel that new topics are rushed upon them before they have been able to consolidate previous ones.

Making sense of information

There is a change in how children handle information as they get older. It is not just that an eight-year-old can remember more, factually, than a five-year-old. Eight-year-olds will have mental strategies

to help them to remember, to organise information and to link it up with what they already know. Some memory techniques may have been taught to them, but children start to generate ideas of their own. Eight- and nine-year-olds already have enough experience to make some assessment of new information. They are partly linking up new facts and ideas with what they already know. But they are also often making a judgement about the importance of a piece of information or the likelihood that it is true, or not.

For instance, nine- and ten-year-olds will know about plants and what they need to live, such as sun, earth and water. Initially they may be sceptical about new information that some plants eat insects or that another kind grow on tree branches and not in the earth. If the person who passes on this information is a credible source, then the children will adjust their view of plants to allow for a framework that has elements of 'most plants ...' as well as 'a few kinds of plant ...'.

Strategies for finding out

Children and young people also have a number of strategies for finding out more on a topic or working out how pieces of information fit together.

- Their first step may well be to ask questions of adults or other children. Eight-year-olds may have this as their main approach, but asking someone else remains a good strategy as children get older.

- Older children are increasingly able to use books and other written source materials to add to their knowledge of a given subject.
- Children of ten and 11 years can have learned the beginnings of how to track down information by using indexes, and topic and content lists in reference books. This skill can grow with practice and guidance from adults.
- Some primary school children, and certainly those of secondary school age, are able to use their computer skills to access databases or to consult encyclopaedias.

Expertise and special interests

All children and young people, just like adults, will have some areas of knowledge in which they feel more confident than others. Some eight-year-olds will already have developed one or more special interests which they pursue independently. They may read books and magazines, collect items of special interest, select television programmes on this basis, or be motivated to make visits to museums or other places in order to extend their knowledge. Older children and young people can sometimes be very knowledgeable about their own specialist area – more so than adults without this focus.

Viewpoint

It is a great pity that some adults feel threatened by children or young people who have gained an impressive specialist knowledge. It says more about adults' shaky confidence than children's wish to impress.

In an individual conversation, one 13-year-old described his frustration, and a grasp of adult psychology when he explained:

'I know a lot about arachnids (spiders) and snakes. My science teacher was getting it wrong – saying things like spiders were insects and that snakes didn't have a backbone. I spoke up a couple of times but he didn't seem too pleased. So I thought it was probably better to keep quiet.'

Once children have accumulated extensive knowledge in a given area – whether this is from school experience or their own hobby – they have an advantage when they encounter new information.

- With a strong base of information, it is far easier to organise what they know more effectively.
- New information can be fitted in and links made.
- Children are in a better position to deal with apparent contradictions.
- They are also more able to approach problems systematically – for this area – because they can draw on their specialist knowledge as well as their skills in problem solving.

So, children and young people who have specialist interests, and therefore knowledge, may think in a more mature way for those areas. If they have a talent, for example in a skill like chess, then their approach and strategies are often more sophisticated than a less experienced adult player. This development unfolds with an able and motivated child chess player; he or she does not have to be a prodigy. The children's experience and interest is, in a sense, carrying them beyond their age in years for this area.

The skills of thinking

Younger children show evidence of reasoning, remembering and planning – all part of thinking. But their pattern of thinking is closely linked to the world as they see it. Children of six- and seven-years-old are still working mostly from what they can experience directly through their senses and what has actually happened to them. Of course, children of this age do not need a given object in front of them; they are adept at describing or recounting what has happened in the past or their plans for the future.

At about seven or eight years old, children become more and more able to think through ideas and events for themselves, inside their heads. They begin to weigh up possibilities or likely explanations that are not strictly tied to their direct experience. They are learning the skills of abstract thinking, which work alongside their abilities of direct observation and talking through possibilities in a question and answer exchange with adults.

Understanding symbols

From eight to 11 years, in the second half of primary school, children are coming to grips with the concept that symbols can represent an idea. This includes arithmetical signs as well as simple algebra. But they are also beginning to understand how diagrams can sum up ideas or a sequence of events.

These older children are grasping that a symbol or diagram can stand for something, even though what is on the paper does not look at all like what it describes. A good example is how children understand that a street map represents an area of a town or city, although there are no pictures of houses or cars on the map. In secondary school, the 11- to 18-year-olds may progress to very complex levels of dealing with abstract ideas and symbols, especially in mathematics and science.

The understanding of figurative use of language is another example of how older children and young people grasp that one idea may be used to explain or describe another in a way that is not literal. For instance, a phrase such as 'his feet were like ice' is meant to emphasise the coldness and not to claim that the feet were literally ice.

Observation and interpretation

Eight-year-olds can be careful observers, although they can be influenced as much as anyone else by what they expect to see. As the years pass they can be encouraged to sharpen these skills and to become much more systematic in how they observe and report on their observations.

Ten- and 11-year-olds can have become adept at planning simple investigations and this ability can continue to develop through the secondary school years. They become more able to organise what they have observed and work out why something may have happened, even to consider more than one possible reason.

Students of secondary school age use their investigative abilities in a number of subjects – notably science, mathematics and technology. Their skills of observation show increasing care and they are more able to look for patterns and irregularities. They learn how to consider reasons or explanations for what is happening and to think of how further investigation could test these ideas.

Undoubtedly, younger children can plan and carry through simple investigations. However, the over-12s are more capable of the kind of abstract thinking necessary to weigh up what might be the case, when previous experience does not lead to easy answers.

Application of ideas

Children and young people may be capable of particular and complex ways of thinking but, of course, they do not necessarily apply them in all situations. The pattern of adult thinking is much the same; skills are often not generalised outside the context in which they were learned. For instance, young people may be able to weigh up possibilities very carefully in a science investigation. However, they may not use the same skills of careful observation and cautious interpretation in social relationships. But, neither do many adults. However, once their curiosity is stimulated, older children and young people can be very thoughtful about the complexities of relationships, either friendships or within the family.

Friction can and does arise because young people choose not to think in an intellectual way about an issue that their parents view as warranting a logical rather than an emotional reaction. An example would be a father's frustration with his daughter, expressed as, 'Why are you going out with that boy? Can't you see he's nothing but trouble?' Equally often, the conflict can be fuelled because young people decide to apply their formidable skills of reasoning to an issue that adults would rather have left well alone. For instance, the daughter might challenge her father on another occasion with, 'So, why do you keep smoking when you know it's bad for your health?'

Similar conflicts can develop between pupils and their teachers. These kinds of disagreement rarely get resolved until the adults, at least, acknowledge that feelings are involved as well as cool logic. Young people are then more likely to tolerate a conversation about the issues involved, because they feel that their perspective is being respected.

Methods of reasoning

The striking shift in development for children of around 11 or 12 years is their growing ability to handle ideas inside their heads with no reference to outside objects or current events. They become far more able to imagine what might happen or to consider events and circumstances that they have never encountered. They are capable, potentially, of organising their thoughts in a systematic way, although they will not apply this ability all the time or in all circumstances. The significant shift that they are making is from inductive reasoning to the possibility of deductive reasoning.

Inductive reasoning

Eight- and nine-year-olds are gaining wide experience in using inductive reasoning. This is a method that starts from the basis of direct experience and moves to develop a more general principle. Some examples would be:

- A bad experience with a neighbour's dog leads a child to be very wary of any other dogs. She has generalised from that direct experience to a wider principle that dogs jump up, bark and are not safe.
- A great deal of practice with numbers has led a child to understand that when you add items you get more, but the reverse is true if you take them away.
- Children of ten and 11 years become able to tackle simple brain teasers in which the task is to work from several items of information to a more general pattern. Examples might be patterns in a sequence of numbers or shifting letters in a code.
- When children have finished reading or listening to a story, they have some overall view of the main characters. They are actively making some sense of separate actions or how this character has dealt with events to reach an assessment of his or her general personality or outlook on life. Children will tell you whether they like a given character, who are the 'good' and 'bad' characters and the reasons.
- Experience of familiar people – family and teachers – leads children to general theories of how a given person, or kind of person is likely to react.

In some of the examples above, children may be only partially correct. Inductive reasoning moves from the particular to the general; the accuracy of the principles reached depends on how representative the experiences have been. For example, the child who had a bad experience with a particular dog may be taking a sensible line in being wary of that animal, but her general principle will not hold for every dog. The principle about adding and taking away is generally true, but mathematics becomes more complicated when negative numbers are involved. In the brain teaser example, children are usually asked to produce the next number in a series or convert something into the code. So, they are being asked to take the next step and use the principle or rule to lead to an example. They need to learn that there are many different patterns, not just the first one that they discovered.

Young people and adults do not stop using inductive logic as they get older. A great deal of science and social science continues to be based on inductive reasoning. There are possible pitfalls in going from the particular to the general, consequently, good practice in scientific method stresses that you must have enough examples to be sure that you are fully justified in making the step to a general principle.

Deductive reasoning

It is not until around 12 or 13 years of age that children start to be able to handle deductive logic. This method of reasoning works the other way round to inductive reasoning, in that the thinking moves from the general to predict a particular event. There is an element of 'if ... then'. Young people in the secondary school years are capable of some level of deductive reasoning – that is, starting with a general principle and working on to anticipate or predict what might, or is most likely to happen. Not all young people find this kind of abstract thinking equally straightforward and, for some, it may always be a harder and less comfortable way of working than using inductive logic.

The use of deductive logic involves the following kind of thought patterns:

- If school rules are absolute and apply to everyone, then everyone, including teachers, should follow the rules.
- If this scientific theory about acids is correct, then I should observe these events when I combine these two chemicals.
- If this is the personality of a particular character in a book, or play, then I would predict that he would react in this way to a given event. If he does not, then I can reasonably say he is behaving 'out of character' and look for some reason.
- If this is the relationship between price of goods and sales, then raising the price by a specific amount should bring about this change in total sales.
- If this is the way in which people react to stress, then I would

predict that certain results would follow if these individuals are in a frightening situation.

Deductive logic has potential pitfalls, just like inductive logic. In some examples, such as predicting the behaviour of people or the economy, there is not a simple pattern of cause and effect. So the predictions from a theory are not absolute. There is also a risk – and one that still exists in pure science – that a firm conviction about the correctness of a theory can lead people, consciously or not, to interpret results selectively so they fall into line with the theory.

Deductive logic is more difficult in many ways because young people, or adults using this method of reasoning, have to imagine what has not yet happened and to predict events of which they may have little or no experience.

Children younger than 11- or 12-years-old sometimes show flashes of this pattern of thinking when the elements involved are very familiar to them. The first example, about school rules, is an issue that ten- and 11-year-olds can be heard to voice. Their reasoning is often linked to a complaint about the unfair behaviour of given teachers in enforcing rules which they do not follow themselves.

Mature reasoning

Some theories of development imply that all young people grasp and use deductive logic. However, careful studies of how young people think suggest that for at least a proportion of young people, and adults too, this kind of logic remains a confusing approach and is not understood well enough to be used much at all. (There are useful discussions of this issue in Bee, 1994.)

Young people or adults who have grasped the approach do not use deductive reasoning all the time in their thinking. The pattern seems to be that, unless young people or adults know and understand an area well, they are far more likely to work on inductive logic, thinking forward from specific items of information or experience. For example, a young person may have a flair for geography and may be confident to work from principles towards predictions about land formation or crop patterns. But, perhaps the same young person is utterly confused by the working of a car engine and can only work on simple trial and error when the car refuses to start.

Young people become more able to reflect on their own thought processes. They will sometimes consider how they have reached a conclusion and whether this still looks sound, especially given new information. They can also be genuinely interested in the thoughts of others, as expressed through conversation. Young children ask questions, often a great many, and as the years pass these questions expand to ones about, 'Why do you think that?'

It is not unusual that older children and young people identify their own logical mistakes from earlier ways of thinking. Adults who have shown an interest in children's ideas, and who do not make fun of errors, are likely to be told these discoveries through the enjoyable sharing of, 'Do you know what I used to think?' An example was given to the author by a 14-year-old boy who explained that two of his childhood friends who were Jehovah's Witnesses were also black. He had therefore concluded that you had to be black in order to be a Witness. This general principle had remained until a more general knowledge about religion, and thinking about the issue once more, led him to realise that his general rule was incorrect.

Problem solving

The most effective learning is achieved through an active and not a passive process. Remembering is important, but in the context of active thinking and problem solving. By the age of ten and 11 years, children have become far more able to think in terms of groupings rather than single items. This shift can lead to a different kind of problem solving, and is essential with complex problems.

To think about:

A good example of problem solving emerges from playing '20 Questions' with children or young people.

This game is usually too difficult for most under-eights, who relate much better to the more specific 'I spy'. Eight- to ten-year-olds begin to grasp the strategies that work in '20 Questions', so that whole possibilities are eliminated by one question. They learn to ask general questions before very specific ones – probably by following the model of an adult or older child who is playing. So, questions such as 'Is it a person?' or 'Do we own one of these in our family?' generate considerably more information for the problem than 'Is it my teacher?' or 'Is it a car?'

Young children are willing, with support, to try to solve problems. However, their ability shows itself within very practical contexts. They need to relate possibilities to what is directly in front of them, often by actually following through almost immediately with action. Even six- and seven-year-olds find the concept of systematic problem solving hard to grasp. They tend to try different possibilities in the order that they come to mind and sometimes persevere even when a method is patently not working.

Eight- and nine-year-olds are more able, especially with adult support, to consider more than one favourite solution and to weigh up, at least to an extent, what might be more likely to work. At about 11 or 12 years children begin to grasp the idea of a systematic method of problem solving. They probably encounter this most within their science curriculum, when they are taught the principle of holding all the variables constant except one – so that it is more possible to be sure of what is causing a given change.

In other subjects, or in dealing with everyday problems, young people can, especially with encouragement, use a similar methodical approach to considering, and perhaps tackling, one aspect of a problem at a time. The steps are very similar whatever the situation:

1. *Identify that a problem does exist.*
   Sometimes this takes time. Young people, and adults too, do not always realise that something is awry or that a difficult situation could be resolved.
2. *Define the problem*
   What is the main source of the difficulty? Why did I not understand or what seems to be getting in my way? Sometimes a mistaken idea is causing a block; sometimes, for instance in relationships, feelings are at the root of the problem.
3. *Explore possible solutions*
   The first idea is not necessarily the best and a choice of possibilities gives more scope for weighing up which idea, overall, is most likely to work.
4. *Act on the preferred solution*
   Ideas will not change the problem unless they are put into practice.
5. *Look to check if the solution is working*
   If it is, then something has been learned and may also apply elsewhere.

Feelings and problem solving

The five steps of this methodical approach look straightforward written down and, indeed, some problems do have relatively simple solutions. However, the more that feelings are involved, the less the process is one of sheer logic. Sometimes a young person's distress at the trouble they are having with a given school subject must be given as much attention as the logical difficulties that they are having with this specific piece of work.

Of course, neither young people nor adults use careful and systematic methods of problem solving all the time, or even most of the time. Everyone is at some time, perhaps frequently, swayed by strong emotions and influenced by the pressures of the moment. These factors can work against the careful weighing up of information and application of systematic problem-solving skills. People may have favourite solutions and insist on following hunches. Some possible solutions may be cast aside and information that is inconvenient may be ignored. So, young people may apply impressive skills of logic in some situations and yet react on a largely emotional basis in others.

The blend of the logical and the emotional should be familiar to any reader, because this is also the way that adults behave. It is a timely

reminder that adults should not expect more of young people than they themselves are confident of delivering.

Individual differences in thinking

Personal preferences

The area of research on personal style in dealing with information gives another perspective on the development of intellectual skills. Young people are developing their own preferences for how they assess information and then reach judgements on the basis of such assessments. These preferences are not absolutely fixed but, by adulthood, they incline individuals more towards one direction in thinking than another.

Dealing with the information

Some people are most comfortable dealing with separate pieces of information which they build up until they are sure of the patterns or linkages. Others prefer to look for general patterns and value an intuitive feel of what is happening or what they are observing. This difference in style could best be summed up by saying some people prefer to start by counting the trees and others with the overall picture that 'this is a wood'.

Both styles are equally valid and have their own advantages in different circumstances. There are, for instance, school subjects and types of problems in which – to continue the analogy – it is very important to know exactly how many trees there are and their precise location. Yet other kinds of topics or confusions need the approach that says, 'This is a "wood" kind of problem' or even 'I think we are being confused by a few trees, I don't think that this is a "wood" at all.'

To think about

Difficulties between people, including those within families, can arise when, say, a parent is very committed to one style and a son or daughter much prefers to think in the other way. Unless one or both individuals make the effort to talk and listen, then discussion can become very heated, as each person claims that their approach is the more appropriate.

Coming to judgements

In a similar way, individuals also differ in their style of reaching a decision, once they judge that they have enough information. Some young people and adults far prefer to reach their decision on the basis of logically weighing up where the information leads and carefully working to be objective about the final outcome. The alternative style focuses much more on the values involved, what is important as a principle or the impact of any decision on the people concerned. The first style tends to focus on finding a logical and sensible decision and the second allows much more for whether the decision 'feels' right.

The two styles of coming to judgement combine with either style of dealing with information. So, for instance, two young people or adults might both prefer to look for general patterns but, when it comes to decision time, one individual wants to weigh up very carefully and the other takes the approach more of, 'Let's do it; it'll be fun!'

Again, one style of coming to a decision is not necessarily better than the other overall, although some circumstances need one approach more than the other. Certainly, social groups tend to benefit from having a mix of styles, since they are essentially complementary.

Any readers who would like to read further about different styles in thinking could start with Keirsey and Bates, 1984 or Lawrence, 1993.

> **To think about**
> Within families, parents may be able to help their children or young people with decisions, so that they do not overlook some aspect.
>
> Perhaps a son is inclined to make his choices in the school curriculum on the basis of whether he likes the current subject teacher. His parent may need to encourage him towards a more logical weighing up of his skills and what subjects he will need for the kind of job he may want.
>
> On the other hand, say, the daughter in the family is facing a dilemma over two invitations for the coming weekend and she cannot accept both. She has carefully weighed up what is being offered in a very logical way but this objective approach has still left her undecided. Her parent may be able to help by suggesting a change of tack – 'What would you like to do? What do you feel you'd enjoy the most?'

Sex differences in intellectual development

Comparisons of boys and girls on overall measures of intelligence, such as IQ tests, do not show any consistent sex differences. So there is no basis whatsoever for claims that, overall, one sex is brighter or more intelligent than the other. However, research into the separate intellectual abilities shows up some patterns of differences. The few differences are described here, but they can only make sense in the light of the points made on page 21. In brief, these points were:

1. The differences are averages and not absolute.
2. Some differences have been found, but are usually very small.
3. It is not possible to make simple predictions from group data to individuals.
4. Different does not necessarily equal better.

Spatial visualisation

This is the ability to deal with and manipulate shapes in an abstract way – not, for instance, by simply drawing them. Some individuals are more talented in the skill of being able to look at a two-dimensional plan and visualise in their mind what this would look like in three dimensions. Another application of the skills is to put together a number of separate shapes in order to copy a construction that has already been completed.

The average score for boys is consistently higher than that of girls in this skill. The differences become noticeable by about the age of ten years and continue through adolescence and into adulthood.

Mathematics

Up to about eight years, girls tend to be slightly better at arithmetical computation – which includes adding, subtracting and counting – and then the gap tends to close. Boys' average scores are higher on the more complicated maths problems that children and young people are tackling during late primary and secondary school years.

Numerical reasoning

Boys do slightly better on problems expressed in words but which involve the manipulation of numbers.

Verbal abilities and reasoning

Girls tend to talk more and in slightly longer sentences in early childhood and, to an extent, this difference persists into the later years. Whereas the boys seem to have an edge, on average, for numerical reasoning, the reverse is the case for reasoning and brain teasers based on words. Beginning in adolescence, girls are slightly better at solving problems that involve the manipulation of words and letters – for instance, anagrams.

Learning difficulties

Although some boys are producing the higher average scores on some of the measures of intellectual ability, their sex is more prominent than girls in measures of academic problems. Boys usually outnumber girls in remedial reading groups and are more prone to a number of learning disabilities, including dyslexia.

Making sense of sex differences

There is much overlap between these average differences. So, there are many girls who are adept at spatial visualisation and a lot of boys who do well in verbal reasoning. There is no support for sweeping 'everybody knows' types of statements such as, 'girls are no good at maths' or 'boys can't string a sentence together'.

Even small differences deserve an attempt at explanation because they are consistently found in careful research. The two possibilities are that the patterns are either:

- genuine sex differences – that would mean that biological differences between boys and girls are the cause; or
- shaped by gender differences – that is by the set of expectations placed upon boys and girls within society.

There seems to be a possibility that spatial visualisation is affected by biological or physiological differences, at least to an extent. One of the reasons for considering this explanation is that delayed or late puberty has been linked with especially good spatial abilities in girls and boys. This still leaves space for an explanation due to the impact of experience. For instance, adults tend to buy construction sets for boys rather than girls, or expect that the boys will be keener to play with them.

The differences in verbal and mathematical ability seem far more likely to have been shaped by adult attitudes towards children and then young people – attitudes which the children themselves come to accept. Research studies also point to the importance of expectations and experience in mathematics. There is some evidence that parents think their girls will be less good at maths and so will have to work harder than boys. They explain girls' success in the subject as being down to effort and good teaching, whereas boys' success is explained by their supposed ability – they are 'good at maths'. When girls did badly in maths it was explained as being due to their lack of ability, whereas poorly performing boys were seen as not working hard enough. At least sometimes, the girls then seemed to be taking on the belief that even a great deal of effort will not pay off, because they do not have the flair of the boys. Some studies have also found that teachers (not all of them, of course) tend to pay more attention to boys in maths – and in science – directing more of their comments and questions to boys, even when girls speak up in class.

7. Social and emotional development

Adults often overlook the fact that children and young people are bringing their developing intellectual skills to bear on their relationships with others, both with people of their own age and with adults. They are trying to make some sense out of the behaviour of others, just as much as coming to grips with tough problems in reading or mathematical skills. To a greater or lesser extent – and some individuals may always be given to less reflection than others – children and young people are trying to make some sense of the other people in their everyday lives.

Relationships
Learning about other people

Young children tend initially to see the world almost entirely from their own perspective. However, they are capable of recognising distress in others and may move to comfort friends or parents who look sad or upset. As children get older their understanding becomes more complex. They can show a great deal of empathy with another's plight or distress. Older children and young people may give a lot of support to their friends and to their family, perhaps making allowances when they recognise that someone they care about is under a great deal of stress.

Children of seven and eight years old have definitely realised that others, children or adults, may take a different perspective to their own, sometimes even a directly contradictory one. Some of the experiences which have taught children this viewpoint may have been interesting or amusing, some may have been distressing.

Ten- and 11-year-olds understand that other people are aware of perspectives other than their own and that they sometimes take this into account. Children become more able to allow for other perspectives, even sometimes to agree with and follow a way of behaving that would not have been their own first reaction.

Young people are progressively more able to stand back and recognise that several different, possibly mutually exclusive, perspectives are operating within the same group – friends, school class or family.

65

> **Viewpoint**
> A mother described her distress on behalf of her ten-year-old daughter who was being bullied, verbally, by a group of three slightly older girls.
>
> 'She kept saying, "Why are they picking on me? I've never done anything nasty to any of them!" She was very upset, but she was also so confused; she just couldn't understand why. I had to explain to her that some children, and adults too, enjoy upsetting other people, and that these wretched girls probably felt powerful because they could see my daughter's distress.'

Recognition of the differences does not, of course, necessarily make resolving any conflict significantly easier. In fact, the intellectual ability to see more than one's own point of view can make young people even more intractable if they judge that adults are resolutely continuing to act solely according to their own, adult perspective. Children and young people's sense of fair play and natural justice can be outraged in this way.

Making sense of relationships and behaviour

In comparison with much younger children, nine- and ten-year-olds are less swayed by obvious, surface information – what they see and hear. They are able to make inferences about what might be or what ought to be. They also become more able to look at a situation or a dilemma between friends from a perspective other than their own.

Younger children are very influenced by what has actually happened, especially if they have been physically hurt or upset. They tend to take the view, 'I am hurt, so of course you meant to hurt me!'. Older children have the experience to understand that sometimes the other person did not intend a particular consequence to happen. They can make more allowance for unforeseen consequences to actions, and can tolerate the actuality that people make mistakes.

Young children are very aware of non-verbal communication and, when their understanding is still limited, body language is crucial to their getting the message. Older children are more conscious of reading the cues, especially of people they know well. They cannot always put their perceptions easily into words, and they may be left with feelings of uncertainty or positive feelings of comfort which they cannot explain. It is probably not until adolescence that there is full awareness that people may hide their emotions, or behave differently from how they feel.

Ten- and 11-year-olds recognise that people sometimes conceal the truth or are not entirely honest. They have learned that adults, as well as other children, are not necessarily consistent and may say different things to different people. Older children, and young people, become increasingly able to recognise and, to an extent, to deal with a mixture

of emotions, or contradictions. The mixture is sometimes within themselves – they may feel a great deal of distress and hurt, but wish not
to show these feelings openly, for instance by crying.

To think about

There are very different social rules within different cultures and subcultures
regarding whether feelings of different kinds should be shown and, if so, in
what way. Children and young people learn the rules of their own group and
part of this learning may be that behaviour within the family is not the same
as that outside. Cultural expectations about behaviour for males and females
in expressing emotions also differ. Both boys and girls will be directed in these
patterns from early childhood.

In a similar fashion, cultures and social groups differ over what is judged to
be appropriate behaviour – for children and for adults.

Knowledge of familiar people

Children and young people have developed working theories about
people familiar to them – friends, family or teachers. They have developed, from experience, a picture of what this person is usually like and
so they notice differences. Some older children and young people are
particularly sensitive to when a friend is upset or how their parents
behave when they are worried. Children notice the contrast with what
experience tells them is more normal behaviour for this person. They
can be aware of an unpleasant or awkward atmosphere at home, but
may doubt their perceptions if the query of, 'What's up?' is met by the
denial, 'Nothing'.

Personal characteristics

Up to seven or eight years of age, when children are asked to describe
someone they know, they focus almost entirely on observable physical
features such as height or hair. They also link people up with social
groups such as the school they attend. However, eight- and nine-year-
olds are beginning to develop the concept of an enduring personality
in other people. They also have an idea of possessing a personality of
their own.

Increasingly, when older children describe others they add some
elements of positive and negative qualities of the individual. They may
use words such as 'pushy', 'rude', 'shy', 'kind' or 'friendly'. The descriptions of older children tend to be absolute statements, since they are
unlikely to allow for variability in the same person.

By 13 and 14 years, some young people build in finer shadings to

To think about

Children and young people can be very observant of their parents, among other familiar people, although they do not always comment on their observations. Adults sometimes underestimate children's alertness to detail. The following examples were given during individual conversations and groups:

- 'They think we don't know if they're worried, but I can always tell if my Mum is worried.' (13-year-old)
- 'I can read them (parents) like a book.' (13-year-old)
- 'I know when my Mum is working too hard. She gets her fierce face on and she's snappy about things that don't usually worry her.' (9-year-old)
- 'My Dad's a pain in the first days of our holiday. He can't wind down and it's, "Let's do this and let's go there" all the time. Then he gets the hang of relaxing and he stops being so het up.' (13-year-old)
- 'I knew my Mum was really upset because Grandad had died. She was trying to cover it up but I knew. I said to her in the end, "It's all right, Mum. I know you've been crying, you don't have to pretend.' (8-year-old)

Viewpoint

Two nine-year-old girls described an incident during the school day that had greatly surprised them. They had caught sight of one of the teachers in tears. They had been especially amazed because this was a teacher who was generally regarded as a fierce, no-nonsense type, with no softer side at all.

They were describing this event to the mother of one of the girls at teatime. The mother put forward the idea that teachers were people and they could get upset as much as anyone else. The nine-year-olds were initially surprised by this thought, but one of them suggested that perhaps Miss had boyfriend trouble. The mother's second idea was that controlling noisy classes was very wearing and even teachers who got cross were sometimes upset by the stress of it all. The two girls looked very sceptical at this suggestion.

their descriptions. They may say of their friends, 'He can be rude, but the problem is that he just doesn't think' or 'She seems shy, but she's much more chatty when she gets to know you'.

The descriptions tend to include possible explanations of why someone appears the way that they do. Young people may grasp apparent contradictions in a friend's personality and be aware of the effect on other people caused by the situation. For instance, they may explain, 'He's a good friend, but I do realise he can be a complete idiot sometimes' or, 'My friend cares too much about what about people think. She agrees with people because she wants them to like her.'

Social roles

Children and young people are individuals but they also have long-

> **To think about**
> Of course, young people can be very firm about the personality of another person – positive or negative – and this can lead to conflict when adults, especially parents, disagree with the judgement. It is important to remember that adults are also capable of taking up uncompromising stances and do not always see or allow for nuances in personality.

standing relationships with others and, within these relationships, they take on a particular role. Part of the social development of children and young people is the way in which they fulfil their different roles and deal with any conflicts between them. Eight-year-olds already experience several distinct social roles. For instance, they may be some or all of the following:

- son or daughter to their parent;
- brother or sister, or a twin, and in families of more than one child they also have a position in relationship to the others – eldest, youngest, middle;
- grandson or granddaughter, which can be a very important relationship in some families, as can relationships with aunts and uncles;
- friend to other children and perhaps best friend to one;
- pupil in relationships with one or more teachers;
- member of a club or team;
- student in activities like dance class or music.

In all these roles the children are faced with slightly different, sometimes contradictory, expectations. These role expectations are expressed in words or shown through the behaviour of others and they come to be part of children's picture of this side to their whole self. Sometimes the expectations from different roles lead to conflicts for children. For example:

1. A nine-year-old boy might feel that, as a brother, he ought to help his sister out with her playground troubles but, as a friend to the other boys, he does not want to appear soft. Different boys may make a different decision – either helping out their sister or leaving her alone, for fear of what their friends might say.
2. As a daughter, a 14-year-old might be inclined to let pass the slightly stupid remark that her mother has just made. But, with her friends also present, she does not want them to think that she agrees or that she is cowed by her mother. So, in this situation, she is very inclined to answer her mother back.

Adults are sometimes insensitive to the possibility of conflicting expectations, and their effects on children and young people. For example, an enthusiastic music teacher may wish a talented pupil to devote a great deal of energy to his music. The boy may enjoy music and want to do well, and to meet his teacher's hopes. However, he is aware as a son that his parents cannot afford good quality instruments and are having difficulty in arranging to get him to all the concerts in which he is now involved. His friends are also complaining that he is never available to come out with them and he fears that they will soon stop asking him.

Children or young people in this type of situation can feel worried, or even overwhelmed by the impossibility of pleasing everyone. Parents are often the ones in the best position to give a son or daughter time and attention to talk through the situation. There is rarely an easy answer but it helps young people if they can recognise the competing demands and work out, with help, how they will manage the conflicts.

Change in social roles

As children pass into the years of adolescence they experience steady and subtle changes in the roles which already exist. Parents most likely have a different set of expectations for a 15-year-old son than they had when he was eight years old. Very different expectations for sons and daughters may be held within the same family and the male or female role may become even more important as children move towards adulthood.

A further development is that brand new roles emerge for young people. When they develop close attachments, young people have to come to terms with the role of boyfriend or girlfriend. These roles may not be viewed in the same way by two young people, however fond they are of each other. The role may conflict with the obligations of being a 'friend', a 'good student', or a 'son' or 'daughter'.

The move into weekend or evening work brings a new role of employee. Some young people can be surprised, even shocked, at the firm expectations that are held of them, if they are to fulfil even a Saturday job properly. For some young people, the work experience programmes in school give a realistic taste of the world of employment.

Young people are frequently faced with sorting out the different demands of various parts of their life and the conflict can become anything from mildly stressful to a genuine burden. For example, parents are often concerned that friends, or boy- and girlfriends will discourage a son or daughter from giving proper attention to school work. Young people themselves may be well aware of the pull in two different directions and be attempting to resolve it.

Sex differences in social behaviour

Apart from the 'received wisdom' that girls are less able in maths and sciences, perhaps the strongest expectations for male–female differences are that their social behaviour will differ.

Expected differences

Cooperativeness

Some studies from Western Europe and North America have shown young girls of pre-school age to be more cooperative than their male counterparts but any consistent difference disappears in groups of older children. All that remains is that the children who are judged to be extremely uncooperative – at home or in school – are more likely to be boys.

Sociability

Girls do not seem to be any more sociable than boys, but the two sexes tend towards different ways of socialising. Boys favour play in larger groups and seem to have fewer intimate individual friendships. Boys' friendships follow a different pattern to girls' but are equally important to them. (More on friendships from page 135.)

Aggression and dominance

The one area in which expectations are borne out by many, but not all, of the research studies is that of the related behaviours of aggression, dominance and competitiveness.

From a very young age, boys have been observed to:

- hit and insult each other more frequently than do the girls;
- react faster and more strongly if they are insulted or hit;
- get more involved in play fighting and rough and tumble games.

Boys emerge, on average, as more aggressive and competitive than girls at virtually all ages through to adulthood.

Although the difference in levels of aggressiveness is a consistent finding, all the tentative points made on page 21 are still very important. The early age at which the average differences emerge, and the link between sex hormones and aggression, suggest a biological basis, but not the simple link to testosterone that was originally suggested. However, this is unlikely to be the entire explanation since observation of parents in Western societies with babies and very young children has shown different patterns in how boys and girls are treated – and from the earliest days of life.

Behavioural problems

There are more boys than girls among the children and young people assessed as having severe emotional difficulties. Boys outnumber girls for problems such as autism, serious behavioural difficulties and hyperactivity. Boys and young men also outnumber girls and young women in most delinquency figures. This, of course, leaves a very large number of males who are not presenting any serious problems and who do not get into trouble over their behaviour.

Biological explanations include the possible effect of hormonal differences between the sexes. Social explanations suggest that greater demands are placed on boys and this creates high levels of stress for some of them. No single explanation satisfactorily accounts for the greater vulnerability of boys. (Readers who would like to explore further could start with Bee, 1994.)

A sense of personal identity

The move from child towards young adult

As older children move towards the years of young adulthood they are developing a sense of themselves that is less 'child' and more 'grown up'. Some young people find this adjustment more difficult than others. Much depends on the support that parents offer and the extent to which the parents themselves are at ease with their sons' and daughters' move out of childhood. Other adults, for instance teachers, vary in their level of confidence in dealing with young people who want to be treated differently from children. Part of the development of a more mature identity evolves from growing independence – more on this from page 106.

The quotations from older children and young people on page 12 show how many of them take a thoughtful approach to growing up. They are seeking a sense of themselves that feels distinct from their parents and, in some cases, more like their friends. The loyalty to friends can lead to conflict in the family, especially if the prevailing views of the peer group clash with the family outlook.

Older children are working out what it means, for them, to be an individual. However, identity is built through a sense of belonging to different social and cultural groups, or through attempts to break away from this source of identity.

Male or female

Children have views about what it means to be a girl or a boy and the expectations that are built around the two genders. As they enter puberty, their sense of themselves as female or male is taking on a different kind of importance, because it is linked with becoming physically grown up. They are coming to terms with all the changes in what it means to be female or male, as well as additional expectations and choices about life as a man or a woman.

Part of young people's more grown up identity includes an awareness of sexual attraction to others. Doubts can set in as a young person becomes concerned about whether they are sufficiently attractive, and most young people worry at some point. For some young people there is also a gradual realisation, earlier for some than others, that they are sexually attracted to their own sex and that this is not a passing phase (see also from page 148).

Identity within the family

Some children and young people may experience greater difficulties in achieving a sense of positive identity, which supports their self-esteem in dealing with others. Children and young people vary, and some seem to be more confident by temperament. However, even the more resilient children can be worn down by persistent discouragement.

Some children's problems in finding a positive identity may stem largely from their family experience. This may arise because they are less valued as an individual than other brothers or sisters, or because, perhaps, as a girl in a family that regards daughters as less important than sons. Young children have a place in their family but this sense of belonging changes as young people increasingly seek a more mature identity within the family. Some parents find this easier to accommodate than others.

Some of the disagreements between young people and their parents, or with other relatives, arise from the desire to establish an identity separate from being somebody's son or granddaughter. When the older relatives find it very hard to allow the younger person to develop, the disagreements can be serious and may cause deeply hurt feelings all round.

Viewpoint

For older children and young people some of the signs of being accepted as more mature can be apparently minor things but these are symbolic of how they are treated by adults. They are asking for small changes in behaviour, representative of a larger change in attitudes. Some adults are prepared to make the effort; some apparently are not.

Some examples heard in individual discussions and groups with ten- to 14-year-olds have been:

- 'I wish my grandfather would stop saying "you used to be such a nice little girl".'
- 'My aunt ruffles my hair in front of people, and she calls me by my nickname. I don't mind the name just in the family, but she says it when my friends are there. I ask her not to and she just laughs.'
- 'Parents should stop calling you pet names, like "sweetpea" and "pudding" – especially in front of your friends.'
- 'They shouldn't insist on kissing you "goodbye" when they drop you off at school.'
- 'I call my father "Dad" now and I wanted my mother to say that, and not "Daddy", when we talk about him. It took a couple of reminders but she's got it now.'
- 'My grandmother used to keep calling me "Little Sandra", because I'm the youngest. I didn't like it, because I'm not little any more. I didn't want to hurt her feelings, so I asked my mother to say something. It was fine and gran stopped.'

Step-parents can find themselves particularly in the crossfire when young people are distressed or confused. Conflict can become that much more heated with accusations such as, 'You're not my real parent!' being thrown into disagreements. Stepfamilies do not, of course, struggle all the time with allegiances in this way. However, step-parents describe how every ounce of patience is needed to deal with sons or daughters whose uncertainties about themselves are being played out in the home.

Twins

Children and young people who are part of a multiple birth unit may wish to have clear-cut identities from one another. Twins, for instance, may have a very close relationship and one that they both wish to continue. Yet they still want, especially as they pass through puberty, to have a sense of separate identity as well. Young people are, of course, individuals and some members of twins, sets of triplets or quads may feel less strongly about this than do others. The young people themselves may have a clear view of what they want but may find they are blocked by the insistence of other people, within the family or outside, on treating them still as one unit – for instance, as 'the twins'. Sympathetic support, especially from within the family, can help the individuals to develop their own sense of identity and the degree of closeness that they wish.

Children not living with their birth parents

Children and young people who have been adopted, or who are living with long-term foster parents, can have yet another strand to their sense of identity. They have a relationship and a personal history with their family, yet another source of identity rests with their birth parents.

The process of adoption now, compared with previous decades, involves considerably more awareness of children's rights to know about their birth family. Some adoptive parents have a personal book for their child which contains an account of their life before adoption. Children and young people vary considerably. Some have a very limited interest in their family of birth, feeling that their commitment is to the people who raised them. Others wish to know more, even to meet their birth parents, although not necessarily with any desire of rejecting their adoptive parents.

Cultural identity

All families live within a particular culture with its own traditions. Children are raised within those traditions and part of their identity is built from what it means to them and their families to belong to a given culture or nationality. The development of this side to personal identity is likely to be rather different for children and young people who are within what is seen as the culture of the majority of the population. In many countries, and Britain is no exception, the culture and religion that has most shaped the history of a country tends to be viewed as the normal or usual way, and other cultures as variations. Families of minority ethnic groups may strive to provide a positive identity for their children. Those children may even have a clearer sense of belonging than children from the majority culture, whose families have not directly addressed cultural traditions and shared identity.

Any child or young person can feel torn between what they are learning and what is expected of them in different settings, such as school and their own home. All have to reach some resolution over the differences. However, young people who are experiencing two very distinct cultures can be, potentially, more torn or confused than most. Much will depend on the extent to which the adults in the two settings, perhaps home and school, are prepared to discuss key issues and are willing to take their turns in compromise.

Some children and young people are faced with two distinct cultures within their home. Marriages or partnerships between people of different cultures bring elements of both traditions into family life. Some parents will have reached a blend of traditions or made compromises that do not force their children to take one side rather than another. In other families, differences of cultural tradition, or religious belief, may be sufficiently clear-cut that children are forced into making uncomfortable decisions.

Family support is likely to be especially important for children whose cultural or religious identity, or their ethnic group, is likely to incite prejudice of them in some quarters. Parents who have first-hand experience of racism may be especially concerned to prepare and support their children.

Values and beliefs

All children and young people will be working out to what extent they agree or disagree with their parents or other adults over beliefs and key values. Some young people find a sense of their own identity by espousing beliefs that are very different from those of their family. The difference may focus on diet, music, style of clothes or political and philosophical beliefs.

Religious belief

Some disagreements in families arise over the decision of children or young people that they do not wish to have their personal identity as enmeshed in faith as their parents' is. This is a family dilemma that can and does arise in many different religions. It will be more acute when the version of the faith, or the family's interpretation of the faith, does not permit compromise. All the major world faiths have different groupings and sects that vary in precise beliefs, even when coming under the umbrella of same main faith, and families vary greatly in strictness of religious observance.

A certain amount of confrontation and disagreement can be one way that children and young people develop a stronger personal identity. Yet, persistent arguments can be disruptive within family life, or within school class discussions. These tend to be avoided when adults are prepared to talk around ideas and explain, without getting overly emotional, their reasons for their beliefs. Undoubtedly, allowing for discussion and doubt can be especially hard for those adults who are genuinely fearful that young people who leave the faith are doomed. This fear can be part of an allegiance to any of the major world faiths and can be very strongly felt by the more fundamentalist groups in any religion.

Parents or other adults, such as teachers, may have deeply-held beliefs, but pressing these on young people without allowing any discussion may get a temporary compliance and silence but is likely to ferment rebellion (see also page 86).

Ill-health or disability

Many of the experiences shaping identity will impinge upon individuals from the outside. For children or young people, their disability or ill-health is part of life for them, but they are unlikely to wish to be seen through the filter of disability or illness. Friends and family, as well as teachers, will have an impact on how comfortable a child or young person feels with their identity. Other people's views of ability and disability can be supportive or a burden to the children or young people on the receiving end.

Emotional problems

Worries

Older children and young people are aware of their own and of other people's feelings. Individuals vary in how much they express feelings, and with what degree of honesty. Part of the variation can be explained by individual personality, but a great deal is shaped by what children and young people learn is expected of them, as a member of a particular culture and gender.

Young people have many changes to face within the years of adolescence, and the physical changes of puberty bring emotional changes and some confusion as well. These years are not necessarily the dramatic time of arguments and storming out of the house that they are often painted. Many parents get on reasonably well with their 13- to 17-year-olds and disagreements or upsets are resolved.

Older children, the eight- to 12-year-olds, are often overlooked in the emphasis on what happens a few years later. The implication is sometimes that these children have no worries or that nothing much happens during those years, except passing through school. Yet these older children often face troubles that they find difficult to resolve without adult help. Some have difficulties in their schoolwork which can affect their later learning if they are left without help. Some children are very distressed by troubles with other children, perhaps by persistent bullying. (More from page 163.) Twelve-year-olds in state schools have to manage the shift from being the eldest in their primary school to becoming the youngest in secondary, with all the many changes that this transition brings (see page 166).

Older children and young people can feel overwhelmed if they are facing a number of troubles simultaneously and feel they have nowhere to turn to for help. Much depends on how burdened they feel in total. If children and young people feel at ease and confident in some areas of their lives, then they are more likely to see the worries they are experiencing as manageable.

> **To think about**
> It takes time and some positive experiences for children to feel sure that difficult situations can be weathered and sometimes resolved to an extent. Younger children, and those older children who have not been supported in learning coping skills, may simply not recognise that they could perhaps do something about their current dilemma.

If young people are worried about their physical appearance, experiencing a crisis of trust with their friends and are going through a tough time at school, then the total weight may seem unbearable. Perhaps they are also aware that their parents have serious worries of their own or are very absorbed in the responsibilities of work. Children and young people can then experience serious stress and feel they have nowhere to turn.

This burden will emerge in one way or another. Some individuals start acting in ways that seem out of character, perhaps losing their temper in class or at home. Some may become physically ill, or retreat into themselves in a depressive way. Some may start to behave in outrageous ways that force attention to be paid to them, although the behaviour itself brings additional troubles in its wake.

> **To think about**
> The time perspective of children and young people tends to be very immediate – a fact of this time of life that adults often forget. If best friends have fallen out then this is an extremely serious matter, even when previous arguments have been patched up swiftly. Young people who are lagging behind their friends in the physical developments of puberty want desperately to show the signs of being more grown up and to have this happen right now. Intellectually they know that the argument will be sorted out or that they will develop like their friends in the fullness of time, but emotionally this realisation is no comfort.

Older children and young people are realistic in that they know their parents, or teachers, cannot solve complex problems in an instant. What they ask is more possible than magically putting everything right. Their stance tends to be that adults, parents and teachers, should:

- take the concerns of children and young people seriously – at least as seriously as the adults are requiring that their concerns should be acknowledged by the younger people;
- give time and listen, with a sympathetic ear;
- offer their perspective and experience, so long as it is given without a patronising approach;

- acknowledge the wishes and preferences of children and young people – or at least recognise that they are not the same as adults';
- avoid treating older children and young people as if they were 'little kids';
- show some trust in children and young people.

All of these requests are evidence of a wish in older children and young people to see a definite shift in their relationship with adults. Parents or teachers who behave in this way are showing good sense and respect for children. They are also putting the idea of children's rights into action (see page 7).

Sadness and depression

Older children and young people have changes of mood – some individuals more than others. Their moods include sadness and distress and some become sufficiently overwhelmed that they fall into a depression. Parents and teachers can find themselves in a difficult situation when they are concerned about children or young people. Adults are making a judgement over the seriousness of depressive behaviour – whether it will pass, how much to worry.

Many young people get very tired and complain about how hard life is, especially as school work builds up. It is not unusual for them to sleep late at weekends – even those individuals who used to wake long-suffering parents at dawn every morning during their early childhood. Many young people become emotionally distressed about themselves or the state of the world, at some point. These are serious thoughts for them, but not seriously disturbing. Adults help by offering a sympathetic ear and by not belittling the concerns.

Most older children and young people will emerge from gloomier times and either pass on to another concern, or find a practical way of directing their feelings. A minority of young people do not emerge without specialist help and their depression continues, deepens and may lead them into self-harm or attempted suicide. Parents and teachers should never ignore any of the following situations. They need careful attention and children and young people will not simply 'snap out of it':

- Persistent worries weigh on a young person and are not lifting despite sympathetic communication, time and attention.
- Extreme and continuing anxieties are affecting, or noticeably changing a young person's social life. Feelings of hopelessness and helplessness that persist should not be ignored, nor should comments about life being pointless or not worth living.
- Depression that does not improve over time, but continues with an all-pervading sadness, despite all the family's or the school's efforts.

- Frequent remarks that show young people have very low self-esteem or see themselves as of no value.
- Young people threaten, or carry out threats, to hurt themselves.
- Young people have persistently disturbed sleep patterns – either continuing difficulty in sleeping or spending very large amounts of time in bed.
- The young person loses all interest in appearance or in activities that used to be enjoyed.

Adults responsible for a child or young person who is behaving in these worrying ways should seek professional help – most likely through the family doctor in the first instance.

For most young people thoughts of self-harm or suicide are passing, doom-ridden thoughts. However, some put the thoughts into action. Some suicide attempts are made in a way that makes discovery likely although not, unfortunately, certain. Tragically, some young people set out to kill themselves with a clear determination and use methods that make survival very unlikely.

8. Moral development – thinking and behaviour

Thinking about moral issues

Children's development of thinking and behaviour over moral issues moves from fairly simplistic views to more complex mature thinking, which tends to incorporate a great deal of 'it depends …'.

Generally speaking, children up to about six years old tend to think that rules are fixed and unchanging, and that everyone will follow the same rules. This outlook seems to result partly from the fact that, at this point in their development, children look mainly from their own perspective. However, their outlook also reflects what adults tell them. Parents, and pre-school workers tend to express simple rules, with very few 'ifs' or 'maybes'. Children of this younger age also tend to judge the 'badness' of an act by the seriousness of the consequences. Hence a 'naughty' act that leads to more smashes or physical hurt tends to be seen as worse. Younger children can allow for intention within their own or other people's behaviour, but the link has to be obvious.

The understanding of older children

As children gain in social experience, and their intellectual skills develop, they grasp that rules are more varied. Not all adults set the same rules, or the same consequences for rule-breaking. Not all children bring the same guidelines on behaviour into the shared territory of the playground – for instance, general rules on how to handle disputes vary greatly.

Children in the later years of primary school are also far more likely to allow for intentions – did the other person set out to hurt or disrupt, or was this an unexpected consequence? Older children are more likely to interpret genuine mistakes differently from behaviour that continues in full realisation of what will follow. However, older children, much like the adults from whom they learn, will start to bring other judgements to bear on a child or adult who frequently fails to foresee the likely consequences of their actions. A judgement will begin to be made in terms of: 'She should have realised that …' or 'He doesn't think about the trouble that he'll bring on the rest of us, and we're fed up with it!'.

Towards a more mature viewpoint

Young people have the experience and intellectual skills to weigh up some of the complexities that arise over moral behaviour and decision making. They, like adults, probably retain some of the ways of thinking that are more characteristic of younger children – such as allowing for the likelihood of being caught out and a sense of personal interest in the outcome.

Children often care about what their parents, or other valued adults, will think of them. This awareness can guide their choices or fortify their attempts to inhibit themselves from doing what they know they really should not. Concern for the good opinion of others and a wish not let them down, can become a more conscious process with young people and perhaps encourage them to think ahead. A sense of mutual obligation to family members and friends can be more real to a young person than a sense of obligation to a broader society.

Principles and ideals

Younger children have some grasp of general principles, when they are presented as ground rules, for family life or within schools. By nine or ten years, and often younger, children will be ready to argue their case if a rule is, in their view, unfair or being implemented in an unjust way. Increasingly, older children and young people take on broader and more abstract principles about life and society.

It is not unusual that young people may take their ability in deductive logic and apply principles with very little room for compromise. They may also take a delight, at least for some time, in questioning almost everything – which includes cherished beliefs of their parents. This single-mindedness may partly arise from enthusiasm for an ideal, but can also have been learned from key adults who have in the past presented their own ideals with strong feelings and commitment. The conflict can arise because the adults do not approve either of the young person's cause or the conclusions that they draw. Children and young people can very idealistic and this can cause distress if they are later disillusioned about particular groups or people.

Young people may well commit to principles and ideals with less attention to practical implementation because many of the practical details of their lives are still the responsibility of others, including their parents. This anomaly is better dealt with by making sure that young people are learning the skills of running their everyday lives (see page 108) and by continuing to listen with respect to their views. Many honest adults can recall their frustration and annoyance when their youthful ideals were met with a blank: 'You wait until you know what life is really about!' or 'You'll understand when you're older'.

Children and young people often have a very sharp sense of natural justice. This perspective can lead them to challenge the way that adults are running some aspect to their lives – within the family, school or other settings. This type of challenge is experienced as threatening by adults who lack confidence or whose vision of adulthood tends to be more authoritarian. Certainly, the type of conflict that emerges from a sense of fairness will not be satisfactorily resolved unless adults listen carefully to the viewpoint of the children or young people.

Moral reasoning and behaviour
The development of moral reasoning

Young people are capable of careful thought and of weighing the pros and cons of hypothetical situations. They become aware that laws change, even within the same society, and that there remains space for different interpretations even within the same legal framework. Idealism adds the motivation for strongly-held beliefs that unreasonable laws or their unjust application should be challenged and resisted. Depending on the forum for challenge, such an outlook can bring young people – or adults, of course – into serious conflict with other parts of society or even with the forces of law.

To think about

Some cultures have a strong emphasis on family ties and, of course, this focus for personal obligation can be more strong in some communities and subcultures than in others. It may well override, in some circumstances, a sense of obligation to the law of the land.

Some of the theory and research into moral development among Western social scientists reads as very culture-bound within societies that value, at least in theory, individualism and personal sets of principles. The difficulty is not in a description of different types of society but rather the strong implication that the individualistic framework is a more complex or higher order of moral thinking.

The aim in this section is certainly not to propose that one or other kind of society is necessarily better. It is rather that different cultures, and the societies within which they operate, tend to take up different stances over the appropriate point to cease thinking over moral precepts and simply direct your life in accordance with them.

There is no reason to expect that the match between children and young people's moral judgements and their actual behaviour, faced with a relevant situation, will be any closer than that of adults. A general principle may well be modified in the light of specific details of the situation or perceived pressures.

Difficulties sometimes arise between young people and adults in authority, at home or in school, when the reasoning powers of young people take them to a different conclusion regarding appropriate behaviour from adults. These conclusions may lead them to make critical judgements, perhaps out loud, of the adults' behaviour.

Viewpoint

Older children and young people can be very direct in their judgements over the fairness or justness of adult behaviour.

In individual discussions, nine- and ten-year-olds have been very censorious of teachers who failed to follow their own rules:

- 'She says there mustn't be sweets in class but she eats them – we see her.'
- 'He says we have to be quiet, but he shouts at us for nothing.'

13- and 14-year-olds can be very firm as they lay out what they believe to be unjust:

- 'Group detentions are so unfair. The teachers punish the whole class and they keep us all back, when they know who it is who did the talking.'
- 'There's a timetable for homework so teachers have no business giving it to you on the wrong night.'
- 'We've stopped going into that shop on the walk back from school. They're happy to have our money but they can't be bothered to be polite to us.'

Adult expectations and worries

Simplistic thinking from adults

Adults who are responsible for children and young people are understandably concerned that children and young people should behave well. Unfortunately, many adults seem to be dangerously tempted towards simple pronouncements about learning 'right' from 'wrong'. This type of approach fails to recognise the careful thinking of which many older children are capable. They will often challenge unrealistic views about behaviour and will cease to respect adults – parents or teachers – who run away from this discussion.

A few moments' thought would reveal the complexities of shading that direct adults' own judgements and their behaviour. Then the warning bells might sound on the high risk of being judged against their own uncompromising moral standards and found guilty of failure or hypocrisy. Total loss of credibility of adults with young people can follow swiftly. Even adults who regard themselves as law abiding sometimes exceed the speed limit or stretch the truth on their income tax returns. The grey areas within everyday life, not to mention the secrets of adults' own youth, can be a serious pitfall to any attempt to be sanctimonious about young people's behaviour.

To think about

A neglected area of study is the quaint conviction held by many adults that young people will, and should, restrict their use of growing intellectual skills to the classroom.

The young people who can assess the reliability of historical sources or work their way through complex maths investigations are unlikely to accept simple pronouncements by parents or teachers. Parents, for instance, are unlikely to get away with the implication that civilisation as we know it will collapse if a young person has a particular hair cut. Similarly, young people are not going to be impressed with parental reasoning along the lines of: I, as your parent, have your best interests at heart when I forbid you, without explanation, to go to that party.

The media and 'children today'

Adults, including parents, are led to worry more about their own children by the public image created about children and young people in general. Delinquent or outrageously bad behaviour of children and young people makes headlines in newspapers or finds a slot within the television news or documentary programmes. However, unless they have managed acts of heroism, young people are not publicly applauded for good behaviour. It will be down to families and teachers to ensure that mundane, everyday consideration, patience and honesty from young people is met with genuine encouragement.

A great deal can be achieved within families by noticing young people's helpful behaviour and thanking them. School staff teams, who have seriously considered this issue, have developed whole school policies on behaviour. At least as much attention is paid to recognition of students' positive behaviour as to how teachers can tackle those children and young people whose behaviour is a source of trouble within the school.

Religious beliefs and morality

For some adults, and within some families, moral issues are completely integrated with religious belief. Some adults may still hold to a moral stance that is rooted in the religion of their childhood or the predominant religion in society, despite the fact that the adult no longer practises the faith. A strong moral stand can exist independently of any religious belief. Families who do not hold such convictions can still have clear and firm values which they pass on to their children.

Individual choice over religious belief

Religious beliefs are one of the issues raised by children's rights. Articles 12 and 14 in the UN Convention on the Rights of the Child describe how parents should provide spiritual and moral guidance, but this has to be within the framework of the developing capacity of children and young people to make their own choices. They have a right to exercise this choice, even if that means rejecting the religion of their family.

This raises painful conflicts in families with deeply-held convictions – within any world faith. Parents will regard it as their responsibility to protect their children from the dangers of loss of faith. Families who feel that their traditions are under threat may judge that the religious beliefs are a crucial part of a sense of community and identity, and are not a matter of individual choice.

For some young people their view of moral thinking and behaviour is closely linked with religious beliefs. Where these are shared, at least nominally, by their parents, then the young people's conviction may be acceptable. In some cases, young people may take up a more uncompromising stance than their family, although still within the same faith.

Parents tend to become especially concerned when young people develop beliefs that are very different from the family pattern. Concern grows when the religion of choice is seen as odd – although it may be a faith that is widespread in other communities or parts of the world. Cults or fundamentalist wings of major world faiths also unnerve parents, unless they are also members, because of the fear – sometimes a realistic one – that their son or daughter's religious commitment will divide them from their family.

To think about

Religious belief and knowledge often are not amenable to the kind of discussion and explanation that may be explored in other forms of knowledge. Key beliefs within any religion are, at root, a matter of faith. The beliefs tend to be regarded as natural and appropriate within the given religion, although they may be viewed as extraordinary and strange by those from outside it. Children and young people who wish to question adults' beliefs or to explore religions other than the family tradition may provoke more conflict than they would wish.

Part three: Children, young people and their families

9. Growing up in a family

There are 15 million babies, children and young people (up to the age of 19) currently living in Britain. This age group is about one-quarter of the total population and is predicted to continue to be this proportion for the next half century. The vast majority of these individuals are being raised in a family, yet the composition of families is diverse and has changed during the twentieth century.

Family life
The changing shape of the family

> The Government census statistics from 1990 give a picture of families. Of all the dependent children and young people:
>
>   64% live in a family with two parents and two or more children.
>   18% live in a family with two parents and one child.
>   17% live in a family with a lone mother and one or more children.
>   2% live in a family with a lone father and one or more children.
>
> The overall majority of families headed by a lone parent are those with lone mothers:
>
>   61% with a mother who is separated or divorced.
>   24% with a mother who has never been married.
>   6% with a mother who has been widowed.
>
> The group of families headed by a lone father was not broken down by the route by which the men came to have sole responsibility for the family.
>
>   These statistics were taken from Woodroffe and others, 1993.

Despite a lot of talk about the demise of the two-parent family, the vast majority (82 per cent) of children in Britain are living in a family with two parents. The differences within society come from the fact that, although many of those parents are married to each other, some have chosen to set up home and raise a family without getting married.

Another broad change has been the greater frequency of separation and divorce. So, some of the families are new family households formed after the breakdown of one marriage or relationship. In the two-parent families included in the 82 per cent, not all the children and young people are living with both of their birth parents. Some have relationships with step-parents and with other children who share one, but not both of each other's birth parents. Stepfamilies are not in themselves a new phenomenon. However, in the nineteenth century, for instance, they were formed after the death of a spouse rather than divorce.

Of approximately 1.9 million children in families with one parent, most are likely to be living with a mother who is separated or divorced.

In the nineteenth or earlier twentieth century, lone parent families were most often created by the death of one of the parents. Widowhood is the least common reason for lone parenthood now. The greatest increase in a kind of lone parenting has been in women who are mothers and have chosen never to marry. This has increased from 90,000 women in 1971 to 360,000 in 1989.

Children and young people in Britain now have, on average, fewer brothers and sisters than their equivalents of previous centuries. The average number of children per woman is now less than two. Lower birth rates have combined with low rates of premature death to lead to a more stable population of children. Children and young people now are far more likely to know their older relatives and to pass through childhood without the loss through death of parents or young brothers and sisters.

Being a parent

Parenting is a role that requires an impressive array of skills and the ability to draw on deep reserves of patience, empathy and selflessness. Although parenting is sometimes described as the 'most important job of all', it shares few of the characteristics of any normal job. The hours are elastic and the job description tends to change without warning. Resignation is not allowed and emotional involvement makes mistakes, or criticism from others, even harder to bear. Perhaps one of the most unjust aspects is that there are usually far more people ready to blame parents for what goes wrong than to give them credit for what has gone well. This is as true for news items and features in the media as for general conversation or within the extended family.

Additionally, this generation of parents has seen an explosion of advice through books, articles and the health care services. Many parents undoubtedly benefit from the opportunity to seek help when they feel uncertain. However, an unfortunate result of the unremitting flow

---

To think about

Any review of advice over the years produces some sources that are totally contradictory, as well as a return to earlier recommendations. Current parents will have experienced so many about-turns, for instance on diet, that they can have difficulty finding a practical set of recommendations.

Parents may be dissuaded from seeking the advice of their own parents on the grounds that they must be out of date and purveyors of 'old wives' tales'. Strangely enough, the often surprising advice from books of previous decades is never dismissed as 'old doctors' tales'!

Interested readers can consult Hardyment, 1995, for a review which confirms that parents still have to make up their own minds about what is suitable for their own children.

of 'specialist' advice has been the implication that parents are never the experts on their own children.

In many everyday situations there will not be an answer that would be correct for all families facing a similar set of circumstances. Parents' best way forward is usually to weigh up the possibilities and try to pick the best line of action to suit their particular situation. It is then important to be flexible when circumstances change or it becomes more obvious that a different line of action would now be better.

Some adults become parents through routes other than giving birth to children. Some gain children as a step-parent, and others through adoption or fostering. Many of the issues are very similar, regardless of the route by which one has become a parent, although difficult times with children can have an additional emotional sharpness (see page 128).

Viewpoint

Some adults will say that they are not really like a parent to their children – 'I'm more like a friend or a big sister.' Perhaps some children like this kind of relationship, but some certainly do not and take the line that parents should act like 'parents'.

A group of 13- and 14-year-olds expressed their view clearly, along with a sense of sympathy for their parents:

- 'Sometimes they try too hard; they should just be themselves.'
- 'Some parents try to be best friends with you. I don't want them to do that; I've got my best friends already.'

Learning within the family

Parents pass on their own family traditions. They communicate what they feel is 'normal', without necessarily thinking that these values, knowledge or ways of behaving are actually part of their own culture.

To think about

Even within a single cultural group, families develop their own traditions that are assumed to be general, until close contact with another family shows up unexpected differences.

Conversations with families who celebrate Christmas have shown a mistaken assumption that everyone does it in the same way. However, contact between two families, for instance when young people bring home girl- or boyfriends, has highlighted unquestioned rituals about when presents are opened and how the opening should take place, how families should spend the day or even whether the pudding should be set alight.

Family members can become highly irritated at attempts to shift from the 'proper' ritual, even when such patterns have nothing to do with the religious significance of the festival.

In some families, the communication of what it means to be a member of a given cultural or national group will be a more conscious one. This awareness is more likely if the family is in a minority in the country or a given neighbourhood. If a family feels under pressure over their way of life, or beliefs, then parents and other relatives may feel it is even more important that children and young people learn and follow the family ways.

Families provide the setting in which children and young people experience a working model of what it is to be a 'grown up' and a parent. Schools can make a large contribution to this growing up through offering pupils chances to take responsibility and show initiative. However, the experiences of school and home are in a different context and both are important to children and young people.

Within the family, children and young people learn how to cope with the range of everyday problems, whether their parents are actually intending to teach them skills or not. Children and young people think as well as simply act; they will learn from what they are shown or observe in their parents and other familiar adults. Children and young people learn, in a more or less constructive way, an approach to:

- coping with problems or crisis;
- managing disagreements and conflicts – within the family or elsewhere;
- learning the skills necessary for less dependence on adults;
- allowing for what others want and for very different perspectives on the same issue;
- facing changes in relationships, or the way that life is organised, and shifting rules;
- coming to decisions and reaching compromise;
- coping with the specific difficulties that can arise through the prejudiced outlook of others or from their ignorance.

Parents vary in the kind, and extent of support that they feel able to offer to children and young people who face difficulties arising largely from the prejudice or ignorance of others. Some parents feel strongly that they wish to strengthen their daughters' confidence to face a society that still does not always treat women fairly as the equals of men. Parents of children with disabilities or continuing health conditions may want to offer steady support, assisting their children to find positive ways to deal with the more negative behaviour of others. Black parents will realise that their children will face racism sooner or later and some parents consistently make very conscious attempts to build positive self-images within their children. Yet, parents are individuals and some feel unable to help in a deliberate way or feel that matters are best left alone.

Children and young people living away from home

Most children and young people live full time with their families, but a considerable number live away from home for periods of time. The National Children's Bureau drew from a variety of Government statistics to reach estimates for the numbers of children and young people living away from home in the different types of residential accommodation in England during 1990. The figures were as follows:

- Boarding schools in the independent education sector   115,000
- Special educational boarding schools   30,000
- Foster homes   34,400
- Residential homes   13,200

(Source: National Children's Bureau (1992) Childfacts No. 2 – *Children's homes.*)

Boarding schools

The majority of children and young people living away from their families attend boarding schools within the independent education sector. Children may leave home for this type of schooling because parents are convinced that it will deliver the best education and are willing to delegate parental responsibility to the teachers. Alternatively, parents whose work takes them abroad, or involves excessive mobility, may decide that boarding school offers the only option for a consistent pattern of education for their children.

Britain has a long tradition, largely among families who are financially secure, of sending children away to boarding school. This pattern has been generally accepted as in the children's best interests, even for those who have been seriously unhappy at school. Parents have not faced the criticism meted out to, for instance, women who combine paid work with retaining full time parental responsibility for their children.

Families of children with special educational needs may find that no suitable schools exist within daily travelling distance. Sometimes, young children attend local schools but their specialist needs cannot be met as they get older.

Fostering and residential care

Many of the children living with foster parents or in a residential home will return to their families. For most, living away from home is a temporary state brought about by severe stress in the family. Consequently, it is especially important that close links are maintained between parents and children, with a view to easing the return home.

Relationships in the family
Happy families?

No family will be happy and calm all the time. There will be disagreements and clashes of viewpoint that disturb periods of relative calm. What matters most is how upsets are handled and that every family member avoids harking back once matters are relatively friendly once more.

Since families involve people of differing ages and interests, family life is not going to be without some ups and downs. However, studies of families have pointed to the features of those who pull together as a more cohesive and supportive unit, rather than experiencing life as full of conflict. None of these descriptions are impossibly idealistic. They show the need for family members, led by the parents, to be willing to give time and attention to each other. In contrast with families who experience a great deal of conflict, families who are more supportive of each other show the following kinds of characteristics:

- Family members spend more time together in shared activities – in comparison with more conflict-filled families.
- They put more effort into spending time together and so avoid or withdraw from each other less.
- Parents and children have many more warm exchanges and less hostile or critical ones.
- There tends to be full and honest communication between family members.
- Family members tend to think well of each other and are less critical than members of conflictful families.
- Family members tend to believe that the others think well of them.
- Parents and children believe that members of the family care about one another and are affectionate.
- People are pleased to be part of this family and optimistic about the future stability of the family.

(These ideas are summarised from Murgartroyd and Woolfe, 1985.)

Authoritative parents
The meaning of discipline

Perhaps one of the most confusing areas for parents in recent years has been the discussion, and arguments, over discipline and the family. Simplistic calls for a return to 'traditional discipline' tend to focus on this as meaning only a sequence of 'no's and doling out punishments – sometimes physical forms of punishment, like hitting. Yet genuine discipline is not something that parents, or any other adults, can impose on children and young people from the outside. Children learn ways of behaving through encouragement, consistent guidance from adults and by observing good examples of adult behaviour. A sense of self discipline and consideration for others then becomes part of how children organise their lives, make their choices and weigh up possibilities.

Fiercely imposed discipline, through physical or verbal means, succeeds only in teaching that those who have the power can force others to do their will. Given that children are growing in physical strength and intellectual power, the time will come when they will challenge parents. That confrontation will be as uncompromising as the adults have taught them is normal. Children and young people are able to turn adults' methods back on them – hitting, ridicule or attempts at humiliation – and they will be very effective if adult behaviour has taught them well.

Britain has a historical tradition of using physical forms of punishment on children. Public debate about smacking young children shows that many adults still think such behaviour is an acceptable way to guide children. Any form of physical punishment has been illegal in state schools since 1986. However, parents or other carers who hit children and young people will only face prosecution if their behaviour is judged to constitute assault. This whole issue has been brought into debate once more because the UN Convention on the Rights of the Child makes an uncompromising stand for the protection of children against any form of physical violence.

Authoritative rather than authoritarian

Neither children nor young people are likely to tolerate an authoritarian approach of adults' telling children what is right and wrong and expecting them to obey without question. However, children and young people are not well served by an approach which sets few boundaries and leaves them, often uncomfortably, having their own way on every issue.

Authoritative parents, or teachers and other workers, take an approach that has been around for as long as the authoritarian line, and is often called a 'firm but fair' approach to children. Adults who act in an authoritative way are not afraid to say 'no' sometimes or to make the final decision on behalf of children. The difference between this style and an authoritarian style is that the authoritative adult feels confident to explain to, and even to put up with complaints from, children or young people. If adults are prepared to give reasons, then they leave themselves in a far more flexible position – able to reverse a decision or to open up discussions in the future, because they can say honestly that circumstances have changed.

Parents who feel comfortable that they can be decisive on their children's behalf are also likely to feel less threatened as their young people flex their growing up muscles and challenge on occasion. Children and young people can be very relieved that adults behave like adults and do not appear to be cowed by persistent moaning from their sons and daughters. Another side to this relief is that only reasonably confident parents are likely to be able to support children or young people, when they do want some help. Children and young people can complain about their parents and family rules, but they tend to prefer to know where they are. An indecisive and overly permissive adult can be as much trouble to them as an uncompromising authoritarian.

Brothers and sisters

Even in generally happy families, children and young people do not get on with their brothers or sisters all the time. Some rarely appear to get on and relations can be extremely strained if there is no choice but to share a bedroom. Children can exercise choice in their friends; they have no similar options about their family.

Young people's viewpoint

All the school discussion groups involving ten- to 14-year-olds became very passionate about unfairness in the family. Those who were the eldest described their hard times. Those who were youngest felt that this was not a good position in which to find yourself. Yet, those who were placed in the middle of families said that they tended to get the worst of both worlds.

The main points that ten- to 14-year-olds made were:

- 'Parents shouldn't compare you with your sister or brother. Like, she got an 'A' for her German, why didn't you? Or, "Don't get into trouble like your older brother!"' (12-year-old)
- 'You get blamed when the younger one does something. They say, "You should have stopped him!" And when you've both been up to no good it's only you that gets told off. Parents say, "You should have known better, you're older".' (12-year-old)
- 'Younger ones don't get so stressed out because they get the benefit of the doubt. When you're older, you're supposed to be responsible.' (11-year-old)
- 'You don't get spoilt like the younger ones. We're older, but we'd like some attention too.' (14-year-old)
- 'Adults don't believe you. They think the younger ones don't get up to mischief. My Mum doesn't believe my little brother can hurt me, but he can.' (10-year-old)
- 'I wish I was older. I'm the youngest and I've got three people telling me what to do.' (11-year-old)
- 'I don't get the new clothes, I have to have my sister's. Then I watch her getting to do all the things that I want to do.' (10-year-old)
- 'I get picked on. My brother and his friends all call me names. And they think they know so much more.' (11-year-old)
- 'Maybe older brothers boss you around because they're afraid of getting the blame. So they try to keep you in line.' (11-year-old)

In group discussions, people of any age tend to get more enthusiastic in detailing their objections than in describing the positive aspects to life. Undoubtedly, some siblings do get on most of the time, and instances arose of brothers or sisters that were good company or had been supportive, for example with homework or troubles with other children. However, the consistent themes that arose in many of the groups, and also within individual conversations, are a useful reminder of the perspective of children and can help parents to reflect on their assumptions.

Communication with parents

Conversations

Children and young people do not want to be talked at, nagged or told off. However, they do want their parents to talk with them, and listen to them, more often than actually happens. Studies that have asked young people directly have produced the following kinds of topic for conversations and communication within the family:

- *Family matters, issues and decisions*
  Young people want to be told what is going on and to be involved in decisions that affect them directly or because there will be some changes.
- *Controversial issues, including those with no easy answers*
  They want their questions answered and to talk around topics, not be told 'You're too young' or 'It's too complicated to explain'. In fact both children and young people are fairly tolerant of honest partial answers – 'That's all I know' – or confusion – 'I really don't understand why this is happening any better than you do.'
- *Emotional issues*
  Young people would like to know how their parents feel and to get an honest picture on matters affecting the family.
- *Caring communication*
  Overall, children and young people wish to feel secure. Part of this feeling is the need to be told that their parents love them and care about them, and that this affectionate commitment does not vary with what the children do.
- *Current affairs*
  Older children and young people are often far more interested in what is going on in the world at large than adults think. They are not all interested, of course, and not in every single issue, but they often want to discuss what is going on and why. They may encounter many current issues in the late afternoon news programmes and within school coverage of news.
- *Conversation about complex issues*
  Young people are concerned with broadly philosophical questions

that may emerge from current issues or from their learning about the world. This interest, or worry, may include environmental issues, religious beliefs, or basic 'why' questions about human behaviour – 'Why are there wars?' 'Why are people cruel to each other?'.

- *The future for them*
  Older children often want to talk about the teenage years – perhaps with worry, sometimes more out of curiosity. Young people want to talk over issues of adulthood and decisions such as choices in further education.
- *Young people's own interests*
  Young people would like adults, especially their parents, to take an intelligent interest in their pursuits. They do not expect that parents pretend they are equally absorbed, but do ask that parents pay some attention, listen and watch, where appropriate.
- *Curiosity about their own parents' childhood and youth*
  Children often enjoy reminiscences that show up that parents had feelings like them and that they made mistakes. Young people are often still interested, so long as they can trust their parents not to go on at boring length about how much better the clothes and music used to be. The problem for some parents may be that reminiscences will reveal how they become involved in very similar escapades to the ones from which they are now attempting to dissuade their young people.

Much like the points on page 97 about families that pull together, these requests about communication do not require complex techniques of family dynamics. They do require, however, all family members to give some time and attention. (The topic of conversations that young people would like to have with their parents is explored in Steinberg and Levine, 1992.)

When parents are worried

Ordinary difficulties in communication within families seem to be about timing and the length of conversations, especially when the topic is one that parents wish to introduce because they are worried. Young people can be far more resistant to one-way conversations from parents who feel they should be talking with a son or daughter on a particular topic. From the ages of ten years to 17 years, children and young people were consistent in their advice to parents who felt sufficiently worried that they were going to have to say something. The main ideas emerging from the school groups and individual conversations can be summarised as follows:

- Say it straight out, don't beat about the bush.

- But please try to pick a time when I'm not doing my homework or watching my favourite programme.
- Don't stew over it, thinking I won't notice you're het up, because I will.
- Say it when you feel it. Don't sit on it until there are 59 things you want to say and they all come out in a rush.
- Don't go on and on and on.

Clear communication

Older children and young people are striving to make sense of adult behaviour in particular. The extent to which they feel they have more rather than less in common with older people, especially parents, will depend a great deal on how the adults themselves behave. Sometimes, the attempts by young people to understand are confused by the fact that the adults are less than straightforward, or show different emotions from those they are feeling inside.

Viewpoint

During a class discussion about families, one 14-year-old suddenly saw her parents from another angle. As she described it,

'I had never thought that they worried about me. They go ballistic when I'm later back in the evening than I promised. They go on and on. But I hadn't thought 'til now that they're worried; that's why they get so angry. They do it because they care about me.'

Very possibly, this 14-year-old's parents might have believed it was obvious that they were worried. But, their daughter had focused on their more obvious anger. This had simply made her cross in her turn – they were treating her like a child, didn't they trust her? However, she could relate to the fact that her parents were worried sick as time passed by in the evening. This realisation led her to decide to get home closer to the time she was supposed to arrive.

Adults naturally have busy, often complex, lives and may choose to keep some of their worries away from their children and young people. Hiding serious worries is rarely successful within families, since children have too much knowledge of their parents to miss uncharacteristic behaviour or reactions. Children and young people do not pick up on every nuance of their parents' feelings, but the awareness shown in the quotations on page 68 is widespread. (See also page 123 on family crisis.)

Disagreements

One difficulty for everyone is how adult concerns can emerge, from the point of view of young people, as interference and lack of understanding. The more uncompromising the adult stance, the greater the chance that young people will be forced into an either-or decision, which will sometimes result in rejection of the parents' wishes or values. Parents themselves sometimes panic that relatively small signs of individuality are evidence that young people wish utterly to reject all the family values, culture or religion. This is often not the case at all.

To think about

It can be very important in family life to try to make up after disagreements with children and young people – and to do this sooner rather than later. Young children tend to move on swiftly, largely forgetting rows or temporary unpleasantness. Older children are more likely to remember, to hark back perhaps, and to take on the adult model of holding on to grudges, if this is what they have observed. It is important to apologise, with grace, if one is wrong as an adult, and not just assume that it will all simply go away.

Every family with over-13s is not racked with arguments and conflict. There are disagreements and some, all the age groups involved may agree, get foolishly blown out of proportion. However, most research on young people's views of their family and parents gives a positive picture. Arguments are usually minor, or at least they could be seen as less significant in contrast with really serious family crises. Disagreements are most commonly over:

- appearance, such as use of make up, hair style and choice of clothes;
- going out in the evening, especially when it is dark, and the return time home. Also, where young people wish to go and with whom;
- the usual crowd of friends or choice of girl- and boyfriends;
- taste in music and its volume;
- choice in leisure activities;
- money and how it is spent, including what the young person earns in a part time job;
- taking domestic responsibilities around the house, such a tidying up one's bedroom;
- use of the telephone.

Children and young people acknowledge that these disagreements happen. They do not necessarily see them as the end of the world, although many would wish ideally to avoid the disagreements. One 13-year-old expressed what many felt to be a downside to their age with the opinion, 'It's a shame, you have more arguments as you get older. About what you want to do, like over clothes and doing things that they (parents) think you're too young for.' Examples of arguments from the children and young people's perspective were:

- 'Your family think you should take care of the little children. I have to take my little sister along with us when we go out to play. But she can't ride her bike as fast as us.' (10-year-old)
- 'The trouble is that you're old enough to do some things, like the shopping. But then they say that you're not old enough to do what you want, like go out in the evening. And that's frustrating.' (13-year-old)
- 'They seem to change their minds. They met your friends and they say, "They're nice; I like them." And then when you want to go out with those friends in the evening, then it's, "Oh, I don't know about that." ' (13-year-old)
- 'They moan at you when you have your music on – "It's too loud!". But if you don't like their music, too bad, you have to listen.' (14-year-old)
- 'I do my paper round and I can choose what I spend it on, but my parents still expect that I'll put some on the side.' (14-year-old)
- 'If you don't like the clothes your Mum picks out, then you say, "No, Mum. Not that. How about this?" And it often works.' (14-year-old)
- 'They say, "Tidy up your bedroom!". But it's your room. You shouldn't have to clean up the mess if you like it that way. But then they say, "It's my house; I pay for it all." ' (14-year-old)

Such disagreements are not the sole preserve of this generation of young people. Honest adults will admit to having clashed with their own parents over all of the above issues. The hair cut or the clothes might have been different; the argument was much the same. Some eminently respectable citizens will, if pressed, admit to having climbed down drainpipes to escape out to a club or to having worn long coats to cover up forbidden fashions.

Viewpoint

One adult, reflecting on her own late-sixties youth, expressed irritation at how much people conveniently forget:

'You would think there had never been any fights over hair before. When boys started growing their hair in the 1960s, it was unbelievable what some people said. How it was disgusting because you couldn't tell the girls from the boys and how boys should be forced to have their hair cut. My boyfriend's parents threatened that they wouldn't let him take up his university place unless he had a hair cut!'

Some young people do clash fiercely with their parents over basic values. However, for many families there is actually much less disagreement over issues of belief – moral, religious, political – than many people seem to expect. Far from despising their parents, or widening any generation gap, the majority of young people seem to value their parents' advice and look to them for guidance and help. So it is important that the potentially minor conflicts are not allowed to sour the relationship, since such a situation may prevent children coming for the help and advice they want.

10. The move away from dependence

The meaning of independence

Different patterns

Families in different cultures may all value the move away from dependence but they have rather different patterns of behaviour in mind as being representative of the move into maturity. Not all cultural traditions regard growing up and out of childhood as a severing of ties. For some, maturity is marked by taking on obligations within the family and taking responsibility in one's own turn.

The key steps for independence in Western European culture have been that young people leave home and run their lives by themselves. The images in discussions about children's growing up include 'cutting the apron strings' and 'leaving the nest'. Independence is viewed ideally as establishing a separate life. In the past, leaving home was not a possible choice for young people who were very short of money, even when they got married. However, setting up home separately from parents seems to be becoming more difficult for a wider range of young people. Financial restrictions arise due to difficulties in getting full time employment, or any job, from the cost of finding somewhere to live and from the necessity to pay back loans for further education.

In cultures such as those of the African, Asian and Oriental traditions, growing up has been viewed much more in terms of a young person becoming old enough to take on the mantle of responsibilities for parents, and for younger brothers and sisters. Maturity is seen as the ability and readiness to enter into relationships of mutual trust and consideration. The obligations may involve giving time and attention, but also money when the family is in need. In broad terms – and there is always variety within cultures – the non-Western pattern is more of a move away from the dependence of childhood towards a responsible adulthood, which includes being part of a family network of interdependence.

Awareness of other cultures can shed some light on ways in one's own tradition – ways that seem so usual they are never questioned. The other practical implication is that different traditions, perhaps different cultures, sometimes meet through friendships or marriage.

Friends or partners raised in different cultures can have difficulties in resolving contradictory views concerning the nature of adulthood. For example, what is admired as responsible adult behaviour in one culture may be criticised as overdependence, or an irresponsible detachment from family obligations, in another.

Of course, not all families within the Western tradition value an utterly separate independence as sons and daughters grow up. However, there is a much stronger prevailing view that young people should strike out on their own and that parents should let them go without expecting much in return. Grown up sons and daughters who feel a sense of obligation to their parents, or who enjoy their company and welcome their advice, can find themselves regarded as odd by friends whose view of growing up is that parents are left behind.

Shifting expectations

Part of growing up is an adjustment to the expectations of others, and how these change through middle childhood and during the years of adolescence.

Eleven- and 12-year-olds are potentially capable of a great deal. In some parts of the world they would have serious responsibilities for domestic tasks, paid work or child care. In Britain, this age group is still regarded as within childhood. It is not seen as appropriate to place adult responsibilities on their shoulders or to leave them without adult supervision for long periods of time. However, some children and young people in Britain are taking heavy responsibilities within the family. Some have become the primary carers of sick or disabled parents.

The development of self-reliance

Families seem to vary considerably in the levels of self-reliance that they expect from their older children and young people. There also seems to be a wide variety of ways that parents behave in order to encourage this development. In some families the approach seems to be more one of, 'You're old enough to do this, so get on with it', whereas some parents consciously coach their children in skills of self reliance from early childhood. In other families, there may be a great deal of complaining about how little the children or young people do to help, but very limited concerted effort to change the situation. Some parents find it hard to be patient when children are learning domestic skills and are inevitably slower or make mistakes.

Many parents are concerned about the possible negative consequences of handing over responsibility – whether this is trusting young people to handle a clothing allowance or letting them go out alone at night. Of course, the point will inevitably come when parents have no choice but to let go. The changeover will be that much more difficult if young people have not initially learned skills of self reliance with a supportive adult in the background.

Viewpoint

One 11-year-old explained how her family worked rather differently from that of her best friend.

'I choose my own clothes and I do my own hair – I have for ages. And my friend's mother still picks all her clothes for her. My friend doesn't have to do anything around the house and I think sometimes that would be nice. Because my parents expect me to tidy my room and make my bed and clear up my dinner things. But then I think I'd rather have it my family's way, because I know how to do all sorts of things that my friend doesn't. One afternoon I wanted us to cook some biscuits together and I was really surprised. I had to tell her everything. She didn't know how you weighed up or did the mixtures, or cracked eggs, or anything.'

The end result is that wide differences exist between young people's abilities in action. For example, some young people are very competent cooks, whereas others can scarcely wield a tin opener. Some are fully capable of taking care of their clothes, including laundering and mending, while others limit their efforts to connecting clothes with the floor. Such helplessness will be very frustrating to parents if young people are still living at home in their twenties (see the statistics on page 11). Certainly, it can also be difficult for parents suddenly to insist on domestic involvement from young people who are accustomed to have everything done for them.

Helping children to learn self-reliance

Potential competence

Older children and young people can become confident and able in the following areas:

- Organising their own physical needs, including food, clothing and personal hygiene.
- Undertaking a range of domestic jobs that make everyday family life go more smoothly, such as cooking, working various kitchen appliances, and knowing what to do about spillages or how to change a light bulb.
- Understanding simple first aid and how to deal with common ailments.
- Dealing with health professionals without parents' presence, for instance, visits to the doctor or dentist. However, some health pro-

fessionals may require parents to be present with young people who are still under 16 years old.

- Making choices over clothes or hair style and cut.
- Handling money and simple budgeting, for instance with pocket money or a clothing allowance.
- Travelling without an adult, by foot or public transport.
- Handling minor crises, like getting lost or split up from a group during a trip.
- Taking responsibility, in the short term, for younger or less able children.
- Helping out in straightforward matters when a parent is unwell.
- Organising their own study, at school during classes and for homework or revision for exams.
- Managing their time and balancing up their different commitments.
- Dealing with a wide range of everyday events, such as getting books out of the library, making calls from a public telephone box or making purchases from shops.
- Facing situations that may be mildly problematic, for instance, taking back a faulty purchase or pointing out that they have been given the incorrect change.

Young people vary, of course, and some are more confident than others. In some situations, which are either complex or very emotive, young people may prefer to have a parent beside them. Yet, adults themselves often wish to have company for a worrying hospital appointment or to feel someone standing by if they anticipate an argument in establishing their consumer rights.

Older children and young people can be very proud of their abilities to take care of themselves and sometimes others as well. Families are probably the most promising place for children to learn all the skills that will be crucial for their later adult life. Schools can make a contribution in many ways but parents have the opportunity to show a full adult life in action. It does not matter that parents make mistakes and sometimes have difficulty balancing all the competing obligations – that, after all, is a part of adult life that young people need to recognise.

The excitement of self-reliance or a burden?

The perspective of children and young people

As the quotations on page 12 show, children and young people appreciate that growing up includes more responsibilities and increasingly taking care of yourself, rather than having things done for you. The greatest attractions of being seen as more reliable are being allowed to go out and about with friends. Being more trusted by parents is seen in general terms as a welcome development. However, the more domestic practicalities are not so attractive and form part of children and young people's nostalgic perspective that being younger can have some advantages.

In conversation and group discussions, a number of points were made about the downside of being older and therefore more capable of taking on responsibilities. An awareness of this perspective can help adults to put a more positive focus on self reliance, whether they are parents or adults working with children in different settings:

- 'You have to look after things for yourself. Your parents don't do this any more. You have to change your clothes and get dressed. You have to do it all now.' (10-year-old)
- 'More is expected of you now. Like I have to tidy my room.' (11-year-old)
- 'Sometimes you just want to try it yourself. They should trust you but they're expecting you'll mess it up. Like if it's something big or important like a video recorder. They think you'll drop it but I think I can do it.' (11-year-old)
- 'You have more jobs to do around the house. Like you have to do the washing up – when you were younger, you just couldn't reach. Now you can.' (13-year-old)
- 'I'm bigger than my Mum now and I like that. But that means that I have to carry the heavy suitcases when we go on holiday.' (14-year-old)
- 'The problem is that when you say, "Can I go out and do something?", your parents say, "If you're grown up enough to do that, then you're old enough to help with the washing up and the cleaning."' (14-year-old)
- 'I have to babysit the younger ones now and they play me up.' (14-year-old)

These comments, and similar ones, were not all made in a complaining tone. Young people expressed the understandable feeling that it would be preferable to be able to choose between the different parts of growing up.

A positive focus

Parents and, in their different ways, teachers or workers in after-school and holiday playschemes, can help older children and young people in practical ways – but only if the adults are aware of how they are approaching the practical issues.

Young people are far more likely to resist learning the skills of self reliance if these are presented in a critical way – 'you ought ... ' or 'you should ... ' – or with an attempt to induce feelings of guilt, such as: 'I would really have expected that you ... '. Few, if any, young people take kindly to phrases such as, 'At your age, you should be responsible!' or simple commands to 'Grow up!' Such an approach is not at all encouraging and paints a picture of increasing maturity as a miserable prospect. If children and young people are to be encouraged towards a satisfaction in being more capable in their everyday lives, then they need to see increasing responsibility as a privilege rather than a threat.

Parents can make the experience more satisfying and less of a burdensome obligation. The key points in a positive approach are as follows:

- Adults need to move deliberately and steadily from taking responsibility for children to sharing responsibilities and then to handing over, bit by bit, to young people.
- A crucial part of this steady handing over has to be coaching children and young people in the various skills, such as those listed on page 108. Adults need to look for, and use, the opportunities that arise.
- Adults have to be prepared to go more slowly with everyday tasks and to explain what seems obvious to them, but is not at all obvious to someone the first time around. Adults – parents or teachers – also have to be patient with confusions and mistakes, including some quite messy ones with some skills such as cooking.
- Children and young people are far more likely to accept domestic responsibilities at home if their efforts are met with warm encouragement and thanks – as far removed as possible from, 'You should be doing it anyway!'
- Young people cannot become competent without practice, so adults need to find ways to encourage them to get that practice, and to be pleased with the young people as their skill improves.
- Part of the learning is also that adults support children and young people as they accept and deal with the consequences of their own actions. These are not necessarily dire, although they may be serious for the child at the time. For instance, spending a month's clothes allowance on a sweatshirt that they later realise looks awful can be a major disaster for 15-year-olds. Helpful parents can sympathise and help the young person with any practical course of action, but avoid at all costs superior adult behaviour – like saying, 'I told you so'. Young people who chose not to keep track of what they will need in school that day have to face the consequences of arriving without the relevant book or their games kit.

Children will not be encouraged if the growing responsibility is presented in a burdensome way. On the other hand, older children and young people are far more likely to be pleased to move towards growing up if their efforts and achievements are met with appreciation, thanks and clear pleasure from adults that the younger people can be trusted.

> **Viewpoint**
> Two mothers described in conversation how delighted they had been to see the pay-off of their efforts with their 12-year-old daughters, who were friends:
>
> 'The school was shut down because of a power cut and all the girls were sent home. Both of us (the mothers) were out at work but the two of them went to one of our homes and sorted out their day. They were planning a surprise birthday party for a friend and they worked out what they wanted to buy. They went off shopping for food and balloons and they kept it within the budget we had agreed. They came back, cooked the party food and cleared up completely. They were responsible about locking up the house and they had got themselves lunch as well. We each got home to find our own daughter settled, offering some of their home cooking and very pleased with herself. It was a wonderful feeling for us – and for them too – that they were so competent and we could trust them.'

Children and young people with disabilities

All the points made in the preceding section apply equally to children and young people with disabilities. The exact nature of the disability will affect what tasks the child or young person can take on for themselves.

Children with mainly physical disabilities may manage well with the support of specialised equipment – although more slowly than, ideally, they would wish. Personal issues such as choosing clothes can become more complex when young people are in a wheelchair. Some styles of clothes ride up and become rucked, and some types of fastenings may chafe and become very uncomfortable after a while. Young people with learning disabilities may take longer to learn skills of self reliance and to feel more grown up.

Parents' own feelings and their continuing adjustment are also a feature in the lives of young people with disabilities. Parents can find it very difficult to hand over the details of everyday care when they are so used to taking the responsibility. It can also be very tempting for parents to step in when an older child or young person is taking a long time to complete a task. Yet taking over will not help children in the long run. These kinds of judgement can be hard for all parents, but families of children with disabilities face additional dilemmas.

Parents may experience difficulty in recognising that their sons and daughters are more mature when those parents are still providing much of the personal care. It may be difficult to judge what would be appropriate independence and ordinary living for individual young people, and to blend the wishes of the young person with the available facilities. For some young people independent living is established with the help of an attendant, but this is far from possible for all. For many families, any moves towards greater independence are affected by the lack of appropriate social services for young people with disabilities. So parents have little realistic expectation of support from outside the family.

Children and young people living away from home

Some parents will not be in continuous close contact with their children in the way that is implied by the preceding section. The task of encouraging self reliance will have to be taken by other adults.

Boarding schools

Some families have sent children as young as seven or eight years of age to fee-paying boarding school with the rationale that the experience will lead them to grow up and be more 'independent'. The word has been placed in inverted commas because this meaning of independence is one of cutting ties to the family for periods of time. It is not the same concept as the one that underpins the previous sections. Undoubtedly, some boarding schools place great emphasis on making children welcome and building a pastoral system that offers the kind of help and support that would usually be the responsibility of parents.

Foster parents and residential homes

Residential homes for children and young people face a similar task to the boarding schools. However, there is the additional difficulty that children may have faced considerably more stress prior to arrival than those children who leave home to attend boarding school.

Foster parents have the advantage of offering a home setting, although some residential staff have made efforts to reduce the institutional aspects of buildings, furnishings and general decoration. However, any residential home will still be a different environment from a family home. There are more children and adults than in family homes, even if residential care staff make efforts to form smaller units within the whole. Residential as opposed to family homes are less likely to offer easy opportunities for children and young people to understand how to run everyday life. Most homes do not have an office, order food in bulk or get items out of the store.

Some residential homes experience frequent changeover of staff. In these circumstances children may not have a reliable adult around them over years who has an abiding concern for their interests and personal wishes. This absence can be particularly serious since children and young people who are in the care of local authorities are likely to have experienced a series of disruptions in their lives.

Families may vary considerably in how they prepare their young people for a more independent life, but young people who are not living in families can be very ill-prepared. They are then faced with a situation in which residential care ends abruptly at 18 years of age. One of the consequences of this is the extent to which young people who have left residential care dominate the statistics on homelessness, petty crime and unplanned pregnancy – way out of proportion to their actual numbers.

Some local authorities, and some specialist schemes, have looked carefully at how to organise residential care in a way that prepares young people to look after themselves. Some have also funded independence schemes of living that cushion the abrupt change. Again, some residential care teams look carefully at how to involve the young people in decisions and choices within the residential home, one of the experiments being the involvement of young people in the selection of new members of staff.

Protection and risk

Parents' worries

Adult life is very different when parenting is combined with the many other obligations of adulthood. Similar situations look very different when they are viewed from the perspective of being a parent rather than from that of the parent's own youth. Situations that were faced as a young person, with the confidence of youth, seem to be fraught with dangers now that one's own sons or daughters want to go out in the evening or attend dances and parties.

Parents can be more helpful to their young people if they retain some clear memories of their own youth. Yet this awareness has to be held alongside the realisation that there have been changes since their generation was young. Sons and daughters are individuals in their own right and will not necessarily want the same things, or take the same kinds of risk. As the quotations on page 13 demonstrate, young people are not impressed with parents who seem unable, or unwilling, to consider what it means to be a young person nowadays.

Adults involved professionally with children and young people – teachers and workers in after-school clubs – have to come to a similar balance between protection and legitimate risk.

Viewpoint

Some parents also have very lively memories of their own youth that have come back to haunt them. One father of two daughters was very specific in conversation with the author, if overly optimistic about what he could do, when he expressed his worries as:

'I remember what I was like as a teenager. So, I know what all these young men are after. And they're not coming anywhere near my girls – no chance.'

The perspective of young people

Young people are often aware that their parents worry. As some 13-year-olds in the school groups expressed it: 'They watch the news on television and they get frightened. They think it's all going to happen to us.' Although these young people had some sympathy with their parents' concerns, they took the line that, 'Parents should trust us; we're not stupid.' A group of 12-year-olds summed up the extent of their understanding of their parents' position, 'You can learn more by your own mistakes. But this can get you into trouble. Parents try to protect you and try to stop you making the same mistakes as them. But you have to learn by your own mistakes, not somebody else's.'

Parents, on the other hand, worry that their young people are not nearly as street wise as they believe themselves to be. Although young people recognise that parents wish to protect them, they tend to resent being wrapped in cotton wool to such an extent that some of them then wish to rebel.

Some young people will, of course, tolerate being protected to a far greater extent than others. Some families, especially those with strong cultural or religious traditions about protecting females, will be very concerned to keep daughters' activities and freedom of movement within what are regarded as acceptable boundaries. Some girls and young women, for instance in strict Muslim families, find that their brothers are just as concerned over their sisters' behaviour as are their parents. Individuals vary, of course. Some young women resent being told what to do by brothers or parents. Others accept that this is the pattern of their life, although they express some regrets about opportunities that they have had to refuse, for instance within school, because the activity or the independent travel involved was not acceptable to their family.

Level of risk

Many of the skills that children and young people are learning will entail some degree of risk. There are the physical risks of learning to do DIY household tasks or cooking with a hob or oven. Children can have minor accidents, as do many adults, in their own home but this is not a reason to restrict children unduly in the name of protection. Otherwise, the end result will not be protection, since young people will probably try to do something on their own, without an experienced adult present to advise if necessary.

There are also the emotional risks of allowing a ten- or 11-year-old to deal with a situation which is not guaranteed to go smoothly. For instance, shop assistants can be very rude to adults, so some of them will not hold back from rudeness to a child who wishes to get a refund for a faulty toy. There is a risk involved, but this is not a good reason for standing up front forever, as an adult, to prevent any risk of hurt feelings. Furthermore, many shop assistants have a good sense of

customer service and include children in this view, so over-protection may mean denying the child a positive and useful experience. Part of growing up for children is learning how to deal with new situations and the risks that come in relationships with others. Every day in the playground, children negotiate the risks of finding friends to play with today, dealing with minor emotional hurts and the re-alliances that are part of friendships, as well as the pleasures.

Learning to make choices and to live with the consequences is part of growing up. Parents need to shield children and young people from really serious mistakes. Yet, they need plenty of opportunities to weigh up possibilities and allow for risks, and then to make their own decisions. The difficult task for parents is distinguishing between when it will be best to offer protection and when to stand back.

Judging when children are capable

Children and young people vary so much that it is very difficult to make firm statements about the age at which they will be 'old enough' to take certain kinds of responsibility. Older children and young people who no longer have to be cared for moment by moment do not benefit from being left alone or without company for long periods of time. They may not need care, but they do need careful supervision and attention.

Parents have a difficult job in facing their anxieties for their children and assessing the level of genuine risk. They then try to assess

> **To think about**
> The media attention of the early nineties on 'home alone' children tended to miss the point, since it focused so much on age in years. The practical point for responsible parents is not a simple, 'How old do they have to be for me to leave them alone?' The more important questions are, 'What do my children need to know?' and 'What do they need to be able to manage before I leave them alone at all?'

the consequences of actions that they took with their children's well-being in mind. Parents may have worked hard to coach their children in the basics of personal safety and self care, but the point comes when parents have to trust their teaching and let their children or young people go.

For many older children and young people, part of the pleasure of being older is the freedom to go out with friends and go to places without having an adult in charge all the time. The ten- and 11-year-olds talk about local trips and going out on their bikes. Whereas some 13- and 14-year-olds are negotiating additionally to get out in the evening with friends. Some young people are pressing less hard than others, but the expectation will come that they can go at a later stage when they wish.

> **Viewpoint**
> One mother described her feelings on letting her son go on his first school trip abroad:
>
> 'Of course, I had to let him go, but I found it very hard. He was 13, the same age that I had been when I went off without my parents for the first time. I phoned my mother and said, "I never understood until now how hard it must have been for you wave me goodbye."'

Assessing likely dangers

A good example of the difficult balancing act facing parents is their assessment of the level of danger to children and young people from two sources – road traffic and the violence of strangers.

In the 20 years from 1970 to 1990 the weight of road traffic in the UK increased by 72 per cent. Yet over the same period of time, fatalities in the 0–15 year age range from traffic accidents fell by 59 per cent. Over the same 20 years there was no increase in the very low number of children who were killed by strangers.

Surveys of parents', and children's, concerns have often shown anxiety about attack or abduction by strangers as high up on the list of risks to fear. Intensive media coverage of the few tragic incidents of abduction has convinced parents that 'stranger danger' has increased over recent years. Yet, sadly, children are, statistically, more at risk of injury or death from people they know, including their own relatives.

Parents are often concerned, realistically, about dangers on the roads. For a combination of both these fears – one based on a far greater real danger – parents seem to have restricted the movements of their children by driving them to school and other destinations or by not allowing them to make trips that the parents themselves may have taken in their own childhood. The proportional fall in traffic accidents involving children and young people shows that, in one way, parents' strategy of protective care has paid off. Yet the unwished for consequences appear to be:

- An increase in the weight of local traffic and associated pollution.
- Lost opportunities for teaching children skills of self reliance in getting themselves around. This will be especially dangerous if parents overlook teaching their children road safety skills.
- Lost opportunities for physical exercise in walking or cycling to school or leisure activities.

Other opportunities can, of course, be created for physical exercise and, those parents whose young people walk or cycle to school tend to be concerned about the traffic fumes that they are breathing along with the exercise. It is possible to coach young people in how to travel independently, but it takes effort and parents can let it slip.

Viewpoint

One group of 12-year-olds described how they are allowed to go, without adults, to the local common. But this was on the understanding that they kept to the two basic rules: 'Stay together – even if you have a row' and 'Stay out in the open – don't go in any of the wooded areas'.

Health and self-care

General health

One of the aspects of care handed over to older children and young people is that of keeping themselves reasonably clean and tidy. Children and young people vary in how willingly and effectively they take on this responsibility. Some need reminding, especially as the changes of puberty bring about a more adult body odour and a consequent need for more care in personal hygiene and the changing of clothes.

Their choices over food will be partly determined by the family pattern and the extent to which they have become accustomed to a fairly healthy, well-balanced diet. Families have no choice but to trust their young people to eat reasonably well from what is on offer for school lunches or to eat their packed lunch, and not fill up from the tuck shop or local chip shop. Once children have taken on most of the responsibility for their own health, however, they may be swayed or confused, just like adults, by contradictory advice about diet and hygiene.

The Schools Health Unit of the University of Exeter reported in their 1994 survey that, overall, girls seemed more attentive to hygiene and diet than boys of a similar age. However, almost 30 per cent of the older girls in the 11 to 16 years age range of the survey were brushing their teeth over three times a day. This is a rate that some dentists discourage, since the potential damage to teeth enamel can outweigh the advantage of the cleaning. Girls seemed to be more careful of what they ate than were the boys, but over half of the girls wanted to lose weight and the proportion increased with age. Their attention to food was at least in part an attempt to diet and involved skipping meals. The survey estimated that only about nine per cent of the girls were overweight by a medical definition of the term. This figure suggests that up to one in ten of the girls would be advised to diet with care, but considerably more girls appeared to be unnecessarily concerned.

Bed wetting

The majority of older children have been reliably dry at night for some years but there is a sizeable minority who still have difficulties. The Enuresis Resource and Information Centre (in Bristol) estimates that there are about half a million children and young people aged between six and 16 years who have this problem. Bed wetting may clear itself up, but does not always, and children may feel very unhappy during the process.

Children with physical disabilities may have specific reasons why continence is difficult or, perhaps, realistically impossible to achieve. However, in most instances, children do not appear to have an identifiable physical problem. Children do not necessarily wet their bed every night, but the possibility that they might can make them feel immature and reluctant to accept sleepovers with friends or school trips that involve overnight stays. Teachers in charge of such trips can be very understanding if they are warned, and confidential consent forms often ask this specific question.

Continuing health conditions

Whether a health condition is long standing or a more recent development, parents, and any health professionals, need to be considering the steady process of sharing, and then handing over, the responsibility for care to a young person. This process can be hard for parents who are used, perhaps, to years of making sure their son or daughter remembers their medication, or takes care within everyday life.

This progressive sharing of responsibility begins when children go to school, although parents will also have had to trust the school staff. Experiences tend to vary. Some families find teachers supportive and willing to listen to parents' extensive knowledge of their own children's health. Other families experience frustration and worry from negative attitudes – either the view from teachers that parents are fussing unduly or a state of ignorance about the condition without any obvious motivation to learn more.

Patterns obviously vary with different health conditions but some themes are common, revolving around careful management of the condition. Parents, and perhaps health professionals where appropriate, need to show children how to manage their own health. This learning process can usually be managed over a period of time so that children steadily take over as much as they can, rather than facing a rush to learn when a situation arises – for instance, a school trip – where they will have to cope without their parents.

Examples of self-care

Children with asthma must learn proper use of an inhaler for asthma and how to keep it clean between uses. Children can learn to use their appropriate creams for eczema or be given patient reminders to take medication for conditions such as hay fever until the point when this becomes automatic for the child or young person.

Children and young people with diabetes will eventually have to take responsibility for their own care. In type 1, juvenile onset diabetes, children cannot make any insulin at all, so have to take it by injections. Although parents learn how to inject their young children, they need to look towards teaching this skill to their son or daughter. There is also the practical issue of preparing children to explain about their equipment – adults who are in ignorance about the young person's condition may otherwise assume that any hypodermic needles are evidence of illegal intravenous drug use.

Even within the condition of diabetes, experiences will differ. Type 2 diabetes has a later onset – in adolescence or adulthood – and is characterised by the inability to make sufficient insulin. Young people who have regarded themselves as without any serious health problems have to face the large adjustments necessary to cope with a lifelong condition that can be managed but not cured. They will need medication and have to learn to balance their food intake and exercise, sometimes extremely carefully, in order not to have serious medical complications.

Parents have no real choice but to hand over much of the care to their sons and daughters, but this is often difficult. Parents worry that the young people will be careless about medication or fail to take care in order to fit in with their friends. Young people with late onset diabetes sometimes feel very resentful that this should happen to them. This feeling, combined with the conviction of youth that they can get away without a high level of care, can lead young people to damage their health – perhaps permanently. Some young people may resist complying with time-consuming and burdensome treatment, as for instance in thalassaemia, and can place themselves at serious risk.

Knowing personal warning signs

Children and young people need to become personally aware of their own warning signs and what possible steps they should take – whether this is something they can do for themselves or has to be an urgent call for adult assistance.

Parents may be well aware of the kinds of conditions that precipitate an asthma attack, or a crisis in sickle-cell anaemia, in their own son or daughter. They will have to alert other responsible adults when their children are young, but older children and young people need to take over this responsibility. For instance, young people with epilepsy may have clear personal signs of an impending fit – perhaps a tingling sensation or an unpleasant smell. With awareness of the early signs, a young person may be able to move themselves to relative safety, for instance, away from the edge of a road, and warn people nearby what is going to happen. However, some people with epilepsy experience no prior warning pattern at all.

If certain kinds of foods, toiletries or contact with plants and animals set off allergic attacks, then children and young people will need to be fully informed so that they can protect themselves. Some allergic reactions are simply unpleasant; but some are life-threatening.

For some conditions, for instance epilepsy or diabetes, young people can take over the keeping of their own fit chart or their sugar level monitoring. This will always be important but will be especially so if the young person's medication or the dosage has been changed. Increasingly, it should be the older child or young person who handles the consultation with any involved health professional. Young people may also be willing to wear an engraved Medic Alert bracelet or necklace, which has brief information on a health condition or serious allergies to common drugs.

Talking about the condition to others

Children and young people are often, understandably, concerned about how other people will react to their health condition. They appreciate help from familiar adults in exploring how they might explain their condition to friends or to the families of friends. Boys and girls can feel self conscious about saying they cannot eat particular foods or dealing with questions about, for example, the effect on their skin of eczema. Part of helping children and young people to deal with their health condition can also involve helping them to deal with the reactions of others.

As hard as it may feel to speak up, young people also need to confide in and trust their friends with important information about their health. Friends of young people with epilepsy, for instance, need to know what they should do to help, and anything that they should not do.

> **To think about**
> Unless adults also share a given condition, they may not realise the subtle worries this causes a child.
>
> For instance, an eight-year-old boy with serious eczema was most distressed by the games period at his school, since teachers expected all the children to strip down to vest and pants. His upset came to his parents' attention because he was trying a range of strategies to get out of games. His parents spoke with the teacher who was happy for the boy to do games in his tracksuit bottoms and a t-shirt. This solution had not occurred to the eight-year-old, since he had assumed stripping down for games was a school rule nobody would change just for him.
>
> A nine-year-old girl with mild eczema was still very self-conscious about the red weals on her arms and legs until a cream was found that worked. Her parents were unaware, until she explained, that part of her upset came from the belief of other children that eczema was catching. In order to avoid this embarrassment she had been saying that the marks were bruises from a fall.

> **Viewpoint:**
> A group of 16-year-old boys talked of how they knew the warning signs when one of their friends got out of balance with his diabetes. They described it as follows:
>
> 'Dan starts doing stupid things – not like him at all. Or else he just stops in the middle of the road. So we get him out of any kind of trouble, then we make him eat something. He's told us what to do.'

Professional involvement

Parents, and increasingly the children themselves, have little choice but to become experts on the condition and exactly how it affects their son or daughter. Good practice for teachers, or youth and play workers, has to be that they listen to parents and children and take all opportunities to learn more, in a practical way, about this condition. Health care professionals should be knowledgeable about the condition in general but cannot know, unless they listen, how it affects each individual child. Neither will they grasp what may be behind a particular young person's resistance to follow what appears to be an eminently sensible pattern of health management.

11. Family change and crisis

Distressing events

At some point within the years of childhood and adolescence, all young people will encounter events that are distressing – the row with a best friend or trouble in class or the playground. Some families and their children face events that are seriously upsetting and directly affect everyone in the family – experiences such as the separation of parents or the death of a close relative or family friend.

The stability of what children and young people have viewed as normal life can also be shaken when they experience upheaval and distress second-hand, through the life of a close friend. Such events can raise serious anxieties and may lead children, or young people, to cross-question their parents about whether they are likely to split up, or the likelihood of losing loved grandparents or even parents.

Supporting children through family crisis

A time of serious upset does not produce the easiest of circumstances in which to try to assess what would be best for the children or young people in a family. At times of crisis, or serious worry, some parents wonder whether to tell children anything at all. A convenient view is sometimes taken of child development that it is better to say nothing either because 'they won't understand' or in the belief that 'It'll only upset them'.

The decision to say nothing is based mainly in adult distress or confusion. Children are often far more upset when they are aware that something is wrong, but nobody is explaining what has happened or is going to happen. In the absence of any solid information, children often conclude that they have caused the upset or decide that matters are far worse than is actually the case. It would not be wise to unload all adult worries onto children or young people. However, it is important to give them a clear picture of the situation that the family is facing since the crisis will affect their lives as well.

Children are not usually protected, in any helpful way, by being kept in ignorance of important family matters. Nobody would wish to suggest that their children should experience a distressing event, as a chance for them to learn this aspect to adult life. Yet, when families have no choice, it is worth recalling that children can learn to cope and they do have stores of resilience, if parents support them.

Circumstances obviously affect exactly what may need to be said, but studies in this area, as well as anecdotal evidence, give a consistent message from children and young people.

Talking and giving information

Older children and young people want to know something of what is happening and what will happen. They can be fairly tolerant of adults' saying they do not yet know, so long as there is confidence that adults will tell them as soon as some greater certainty emerges.

Children and young people can be very uneasy if they feel confused about how their life may change. They have their own rituals of everyday life and they usually want some reassurance that what is important to them will not be turned upside down. If there will be changes, such as moving home after a divorce, they want to know and to be consulted. If there are financial difficulties, arising from unemployment or serious troubles within the family business, then children need to know that this is the source of their parents' worries. Otherwise they may assume that their family is about to split up.

Listening to children and young people

Children want to be told what is happening, but they will also have their own questions and feelings about family upheaval of any kind. Some children and young people want to talk more than others, but all of them need to feel that adults would listen if asked.

One of the sadder aspects of some studies of the aftermath of divorce has been that many of the children and young people interviewed have said that these interviews were the first time that anyone had showed a real interest in how they felt. Children's feelings can be respected and considered, even when what they would most wish is not possible.

Relieving children of inappropriate stress

Children and young people can be very sensitive to the feelings of adults, although their perspective can be different. It is important that adults do not thoughtlessly imply that children are silly or cannot possibly understand. Young people and children can be supportive to parents experiencing worries, so long as they are not overburdened – for example, perhaps with a parent's grief over bereavement.

Children and young people wish to be informed but do not want to be weighed down by stresses that they cannot resolve. They should not be expected to take sides in the breakdown of a relationship or marriage. Adults need to remember that children can still love both parents when the adults themselves feel nothing but anger or frustration towards each other. The adults' feelings are their responsibility, to be sorted out – as far as humanly possible – without dragging in the children.

Continuing with normal life

Everyday routine can be a support in times of crisis and children's normal lifestyles should not be disrupted more than necessary. Holding on to what does not have to change is not the same as pretending that nothing has happened. For example, children do not need to know all the details of financial problems in the family, but they do need to be involved in how this crisis will affect what has been normal family life so far.

Separation and divorce

This type of family crisis is not a single event. A key point about separation and divorce is the distressing effects of the family conflict that so often runs up to a final decision to end the relationship.

Family conflict

Persistent and disruptive conflict is not the same as an occasional disagreement. The latter can be an opportunity for children to see that adults can apologise, make up and discuss whatever was the source of the argument when the two parties have calmed down. Generally speaking, however, children and young people do not like their parents to argue. Many children in two-parent families now will have at least some friends whose parents have divorced. This awareness can lead them to be worried that arguments inevitably escalate into the breakdown of a relationship.

A continuing and persistent pattern of conflict – whether this is loud rows or cold unpleasant silences interspersed with argument – has a damaging effect on children. Children, even more than young people, cannot escape the pernicious atmosphere when it is in their own home. Even young people, with more options for leaving the house and organising their own leisure time, can be badly affected by the lack of a calm and friendly home to which to return.

Divorce is a process that stretches over time. Perhaps, like bereavement, it can never be completely over, because it has brought about an irrevocable change in family life. The events will have shaped children and young people's view of adult life, not necessarily with grim consequences, but there has been a major change.

Allowing for children's views

Separation and divorce can be a very distressing time for the adults, and trying to allow for the feelings and wants of children may seem very hard. The developments in a mediation service for separating

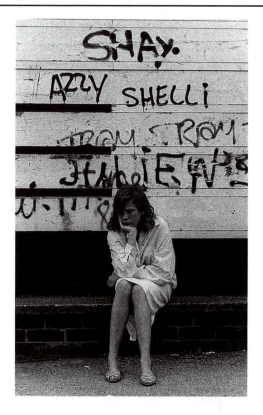

couples include making sure that children and young people are heard within the process. Their views can all too easily become lost in an acrimonious court battle. Children and young people will have views and strong preferences that should be respected: over their living arrangements, visiting the non-custodial parent and later issues such as their surname if their mother remarries.

It has to be guesswork as to the likely experience for the children if the original two adults had stayed together solely 'for the sake of the children'. Research has generally concentrated on families that either remain intact or break apart, and has not identified how happy a family is staying together. Certainly, in general discussion some young people, and adults, do not express much gratitude to parents who stayed under the same roof but created a miserable atmosphere of constant rows or poisonous silences.

Children and young people may feel very strongly about keeping in touch with parts of the family that have become estranged through divorce. They usually want contact with the non-custodial parent, and to have this contact as calm and free of aggravation as possible. However, children are also likely to want continued and friendly contact with other relatives and not to lose half their extended family through the separation of their parents.

New families and adjustments

Lone parenting

Lone parents, like any parents, are a varied group. Some, who have lost a partner through the breakdown of a relationship, or less frequently through bereavement, will be adjusting with sadness to life without that other person. Some lone parents are relieved to have ended a distressing or violent relationship. A growing subgroup (see page 91) have chosen motherhood without marriage and, in some cases, without ever living with the children's father.

Raising children is a time-consuming and expensive life task and lone mothers or fathers can find themselves short of money or with less emotional support than would be ideal for any parent. Much depends on the financial and emotional support that is available from the non-residential parent. Children usually want to maintain contact with the non-residential parent, who is also usually the non-custodial parent, although shared custody arrangements are sometimes made. Children can learn to move relatively happily between two households, but much depends on how hard the parents work to ease this relationship. Disagreements between the adults can spill over into children's lives – and the children can, of course, set one parent against another for their own interests.

Further adjustments have to be made when lone parents develop new relationships. Children may find it difficult to accept a new partner into their home, but they can also object when the non-residential parent finds a new partner and time has to be shared with that other person. Young people who are coming to terms with their own sexual awareness may not wish to face their parents' adult sexual needs.

New relationships require adjustments but are not always a source of serious difficulties. Some children and young people can be relieved that a parent, who they know has been lonely, has found someone who cares for him or her.

Stepfamilies

Some relationships develop into new family households. In 1991 there were 770,000 under-sixteens living full time in stepfamilies. An additional 280,000 children were sons or daughters born to the new couple. (Figures are from the Stepfamily Fact File 1.)[1] Of the children who live full time in stepfamilies, the majority experienced this change between their fourth and tenth birthdays. Other children, the exact numbers are unknown, are resident elsewhere but will visit the stepfamilies.

1 Stepfamily Fact File 1 is available from Stepfamily Publications, Chapel House, 18 Hatton Place, London EC1 8RU.

New family households require adjustments and some stepfamilies experience difficulties. It can be hard for even careful studies to assess whether stepfamilies experience greater problems overall than those families which include two birth parents and their own children. Certainly some stepfamilies describe serious problems of adjustment with children or with previous partners. Children and young people, who may be feeling that their life has been unfairly disrupted, can have a rich vein of confused, or guilty, adults to set one against another. This source can only be made to dry up if the adults communicate well together and sink their differences as far as possible.

Viewpoint

A father in his forties and his second wife explained how they had tried to achieve a calm atmosphere for his daughters:

'I disagree with my first wife on many things and how she raises the girls is one of them. But we've tried very hard never to criticise the girls' mother in front of them. There have been a lot of differences in the way we want my daughters to behave in our home. So we've taken the line of, "This is the way we do it here. In your Mum and Dave's (stepfather) house, they run it their way." And it has worked out, mainly I think because the girls know where they are and they certainly like coming here.'

Stepfamilies can give rise to a mix of roles, even more so than in birth families. One adult can be a parent to some children, a step-parent to others, a partner to one adult and an ex-partner to another. There will be many more grandparents and other relatives. Even when family members are clear about relationships and see no serious problems, people outside the family can sometimes complicate the situation by making heavy weather out of grasping how individuals are related to each other.

Stepfamilies share many of the same practical issues as birth families, but with some extra emotional tensions over potential conflicts and loyalties. There can be the practical, and emotive, issue of what children call a step-parent, since their birth parent may understandably object to sharing 'Dad' or 'Mum'. Families have to decide on what is best for them, with the full involvement of the children and what they would prefer. Given that much of society is more informal, some step-parents are called by their first name. Families have to sort out issues of parental authority and key decisions about children. There can be a certain amount of bargaining between two households and adjustment to different households' rules, but many stepfamilies manage to work this out.

Step-parents may sometimes feel that fairly normal disagreements with young people are caused directly by the family situation. A young person may throw that issue at the parents, but, in other circumstances, it could well have been something else. Only talking through the current situation is likely to unravel what can genuinely be explained in terms of the family make-up and which difficulties are shared with many families who have sons or daughters of this age.

A poor relationship between step- or half-brothers and sisters can be seen as evidence that stepfamilies themselves are the disruptive force. However, some brothers and sisters who share both parents and are living in their birth families, have ferocious rows. Nobody suggests that this enmity proves that children should not be raised in families.

Step-parents are likely to need even larger resources of patience and understanding than adults living with children to whom they are the birth parents. In some although not all family situations, a new step-parent may face wariness or outright hostility from children who resent making emotional space for another person, let alone physical space in the home. Allegiances can become fraught. For instance, some children and young people believe that, in an argument, their birth parent should always side with them and not with their step-parent.

Children and young people, with the full support of the adults involved, can adjust to new families or to moving, in a predictable pattern, between two households. A new life develops, although many children in the early stages of adjustment say that, ideally, they wish their parents had not broken up in the first place.

Divided households and stepfamilies can lead to a more complex set of relationships and some very mixed feelings. However, the most positive approach to making new families work seems to be much the same as with any family. The lines of communication need to be kept open between the adults, and children need to be involved fully. As with any family, there is the continuing issue of separating adult views and frustrations from the needs, welfare and preferences of the children.

Death and bereavement

The experience of loss

Several generations ago in Britain, it was very likely that children would experience the death of young brothers or sisters from serious childhood illness. It was far more usual for children to lose a parent – fathers in wartime conflict, mothers from complications of childbirth, and either parent from serious illness. Improved medical care and the absence of a major war has led to a situation in which many children do not experience death in a way that is personally close to them. They may reach adolescence or even adulthood before they start to lose grandparents. This change means that most children are spared the heart-breaking losses of previous generations. But, it has left adults confused over how best to support those children, and their families, who are bereaved.

The general suggestions about coping with distress in the family, (see page 123), hold for the experience of bereavement. They are also equally applicable for dealing with the serious stress that families go through when an adult or child has a life-threatening illness or serious disability. Parents, and children, are individuals and families have to find the way that best suits them. However, it is not helpful in the long run to decide to leave children or young people out of conversations about what is happening. It is an experience of the family and the family needs to get through it together.

Children's understanding and feelings

Older children, of eight to 12 years of age, understand that death means that someone is gone forever. Their reactions of grief can affect their life, including school work, just as is the case with adults and young people. Children vary in how much, and in what way, they wish to talk about their loss, but most will want some conversation, rather than to behave as if nothing important has happened. Neither children, nor young people, usually wish to be an uncomfortable centre of attention at school. They usually welcome discreet sympathy and probably the effort by teachers to tell their classmates what has happened, so the children themselves do not have to keep explaining.

The over-eights are old enough to wonder and worry about what will happen to the family after the death of a parent, or how the loss of a loved grandparent or other relative will change their lives. Children and young people need reassurance and clear communication about what is happening or is likely to happen. Their grief needs to be acknowledged and adults should not assume that, just because a child says very little, she or he is untouched by the loss.

Young people can experience very mixed emotions. In their development they are moving towards feeling more grown-up, less dependent on adults, and yet their loss can make them feel suddenly more dependent and arouse uncertainties. At the very time they wish for home to be the place that is more predictable, their sense of security can be jolted by this loss. The loss of a parent may make them feel that perhaps they should step in for the remaining parent. However, the loss of a brother or sister can make them equally concerned about how they should support other members of the family and confused about how, practically, to help. Young people may wish to talk within their own family, but some are more comfortable expressing their feelings to friends or to other, trusted adults.

Some families lose adults, or children, after serious illness or the physical effects of disability. They are then facing loss after a short, or lengthy, distressing experience of watching a loved one become progressively more ill. Such a period can be very stressful on all the family and, again, some adults are inclined to attempt to shield children from reality. Generally it is better to be honest with children and young people, although possibly brief about the details. Some units that specialise in the treatment of very sick or disabled children have a policy of involving other children in the family and talking with them.

Children and their families experience a different kind of loss when babies die for unexplained causes – described as cot death or sudden infant death syndrome (SIDS). Such deaths are unexpected and the circumstances surrounding the event are traumatic. The distress of the parent who discovers the death is followed swiftly by the arrival of the emergency services of ambulance and police. Children as well as parents can be seriously distressed by the panic and shock – overnight the family's world has changed.

The process of bereavement

Cultures vary considerably in the rituals that are built around death and grieving. In Britain generally there has been a certain loss of ritual around the process of death and an increased uncertainty about how best to deal with the situation – both immediately and as time passes. Families have to find what is best for them. For some it helps to have a special time on the anniversary of a loved person's death or their birthday. Other families want to share memories when they all feel like it, perhaps looking at photos or home videos and remembering their time together, as well as their loss.

Individual adults who have experienced loss can react in quite different ways, so it is not surprising that children and young people do not follow a consistent or prescribed pattern. Individuals who say very little are not necessarily unmoved by what has happened. Everyone may wish to express their feelings of sorrow, but people do this in different ways. It is perhaps most important for those on the sidelines, and wishing to be supportive, to ask how they can help rather than push a specific kind of support. The other important issue is to realise that bereavement is a long steady process and children, young people and adults are not neatly 'over it' by a given time.

Part four: Children and young people in society

Part of growing up through childhood is the amount of time spent out of the home, or in activities and relationships that are not directly linked with family life. Parents and children who talk together can have a fairly detailed understanding of what they each do in the hours apart. Children and young people often wish to know what their parents do – not in enormous detail, but many of them are interested.

Children increasingly apply their social and other skills in a range of settings, with friends as well as family. They encounter different sets of expectations and pressures and may often view a situation, perhaps the requirements of school, in a rather different way to their parents.

12. Friendships

Friends can be very important in the lives of children and young people. The development of friendships offers a context outside the family, as children develop a sense of themselves as individuals with likes and dislikes and patterns of interests. Younger children want friends to come and play at their home. Older children and young people may still wish to invite friends back home, but their activities now extend to shared interests which are often pursued without an accompanying adult.

Patterns in friendship

Children and young people are individuals, so their friendships do not follow an identical pattern. However, research into children's friendships has highlighted a number of consistent findings. This section covers the main points and further information can be found in Bee, 1994, or Cobb, 1992.

The following features are common for friendships from late childhood:

- Children may have circles of friends, with some being closer friends than others.
- Friendships seem to be fairly stable; they last months and sometimes years – not just a matter of weeks.

Viewpoint

A 12-year-old girl commented in conversation about how friendships change as you get older:

'In the infants when we wanted somebody to do something, we would say, "I'll be your best friend", like it was a prize. You can see the strength of friendship, and the want of it, because 99 per cent of people would say "OK". We'd never do that now.'

- Friends do sometimes argue and make up. Sometimes they drift apart, perhaps because they are in different classes in school, but may become close again later.
- Many friendships are based on shared interests and are consolidated as children spend time together. Some of these friendships cross family differences of culture or religion, or of ethnic group, as may some partnerships later.

Viewpoint

A girl aged nine years described how, for her, different family patterns were thrown into relief by her friendship with another girl:

'In my family we talk about all sort of things and we don't always agree. But my parents say that you can like somebody a lot, but you don't both like the same things. I try to explain this to my best friend, because she gets all worried when we disagree. Like with music, she gets worked up and says, "Do you mind that I don't really like your favourite group?" I explain that of course I don't mind; but I don't think she believes me.'

- Friends try to resolve disagreements, probably more by talk as they get older, including some way of apologising.
- In childhood the close friendships are more usually single sex, although not always. This pattern may arise because of the different interests and activities of boys and girls. An additional reason appears to be the social pressure from other children against boy-girl friendships.

Viewpoint

A ten-year-old expressed her frustration about the attitudes of other children:

'I'm good friends with Matt. We go to tea at each other's houses, we go to the park. That kind of thing. The other kids are stupid sometimes, mainly the boys. They say, "You love Matt" or "When's he going to ask you out?" They're stupid; they can't understand that he's just my friend.'

Groups of children may be mixed sex but individual children who choose to spend time with a member of the opposite sex can encounter a lot of teasing. In the later years of primary school some boys and girls may form a friendly group, who share at least some activities. By 13- and 14-years-old, some, but certainly not all, young people show more interest in going around in mixed-sex groups. Informal meetings

between the sexes involve a certain amount of teasing and verbal challenge.

Some young people may not be permitted to mix with members of the opposite sex who are not part of the family. Strict Muslim families, for example, will be very concerned that girls should not meet boys informally.

Sex differences within friendships

Studies of the friendships of children and young people have shown slightly different patterns for boys and girls. Friendships are equally important for both sexes but broad differences emerge in how the friendship unfolds and what is most valued. (The books suggested on page 135 will also be useful for a review of this aspect of friendship.)

Talking together

Girls' friendships tend to involve a great deal of talking together and sharing confidences as an activity within the friendship. Boys talk together, but their conversations tend to be more about concrete events. Their shared time is focused more on the physical activities that absorb them or on interests such as playing computer games.

Anecdotal evidence suggests that telephone bills are more under threat from daughters than sons. Girls over 12 years can spend long periods chatting on the phone, whereas the boys tend to be more focused on specific messages – 'What's the homework?' 'When are we meeting?' 'You won't forget the game you promised to lend me?' – than general conversation.

Loyalty and intimacy

Both the sexes feel these qualities to be important in friendships, along with trust. Boys and girls feel that friends should be reliable and stand by each other in times of trouble or in the face of a threat from other children. Both boys and girls seem to seek security through their friendships but the pattern is not the same for both sexes.

As girls move from childhood into adolescence they want to be able to trust a friend with confidences. Some of the most common stresses in female friendships arise from not keeping confidences, talking behind a friend's back and being unreliable in the support of friends – for instance by not speaking up for them.

Boys seem to be just as close emotionally to their male friends but they achieve this intimacy in a different way from girls. Boys spend less time talking about their feelings than girls of the same age and the focus is more on sharing activities that cement the friendship. For example, conversations may be about the detail of team games such as football. Since the explosion of computer games, boys' conversations tend to include detailed discussions of games systems, sharing information on the hidden cheats and voicing opinions of the relative merits and frustrations of different games.

Probably because boys do not share personal information in the same way as girls, they are less concerned about the risk of broken confidences. Their focus on loyalty and trust requires friends to stand by one another – physically if necessary – and that they maintain silence when adults press to know who did some reprehensible deed.

Viewpoint

A mother commented on the different patterns displayed by her son and daughter when each had a friend whose parents were divorcing:

'My daughter and her friends were only eight or nine at the time and they were very supportive of Louise. They were concerned about her and talked in their small group about what was going on and how Louise felt.

At about the same age, my son had announced over lunch one day that, "Jon says his parents are getting divorced". I asked him if they had talked about it and how did Jon feel. My son looked at me as if I had gone loopy – "We don't talk about that kind of stuff, Mum. Jon said his parents were getting divorced, we said, 'Oh' and that was it."'

Spending time with friends

Playing

The kinds of games change, but play continues well into adolescence and merges with young people's leisure pursuits. Older children are still playing make believe games or getting involved in physically active chasing games. Increasingly they are able to play different team games with rules, sometimes adapting the games to suit for the situation and number of players. They also become more able to deal with board or card games without an adult present. Older children, compared with the younger age groups, are able to organise themselves to play, whether at someone's house or going out into the local neighbourhood.

Viewpoint

In group discussions, children of ten and 11 years old, often pointed to their greater freedom to go out with their friends as one of the changes that was good about being their age. It was evidence of trust that they did not always have to have an adult with them, although some outings and going out after dark were still being supervised by parents in some families.

Being together

Young people may pursue specific activities in each other's company, but increasingly they simply spend time together. Sometimes this will have a clear focus, such as going to a dance or party. Young people will often use the fact that they are with company to calm their parents' worries about their going out in the evening.

However, friends often enjoy the kind of apparently aimless 'hanging around' that adults seem to forget is an activity in its own right. This shared time together may be focused on listening to music, or going into town or sitting in a big group on the local common and just talking – with or without background music. Adults sometimes overreact to young people's tendency to 'hang around' in groups. A group of a dozen or so young people may form a blockage on the pavement or look like a major gathering on the common, yet the majority of such groups are innocent and not involved in any kind of troublemaking.

Adults have a realistic and legitimate concern about street corner groups of young people who are selling and passing on drugs. However, there is no basis for assuming that every group is part of a local drug culture. Many young people on streets and in shopping centres are doing nothing much at all – but in a companionable way. They are talking, grumbling, staring, wandering around, hoping that something interesting might just happen, and, in single sex groups, making sure that their paths cross those of the opposite sex.

Children with disabilities

Much more has been written about play with young children who have disabilities than on practical suggestions for leisure activities for older children and young people. The older age groups can, of course, become very bored if they have little to occupy them, and the risk is then that children and young people with disabilities may be trapped within repetitive activities that fail to interest or stretch them. Difficulties in behaviour can then follow, largely as a consequence of the boredom.

Children's interests and their range of abilities will, naturally, direct the most sensible choice of leisure pursuits. They will also be affected by the extent to which the various activities welcome children with disabilities or even make their inclusion possible – this involves practical issues such as access.

Physical disabilities may shape the kind of activities that are either possible or enjoyable to a child, and learning disabilities may mean that teaching young people activities such as board or card games needs to be handled in a series of manageable steps. (See, for instance, Jeffree and Cheseldine, 1984.)

Children with disabilities have the same broad range of interests as any other group of children and young people. It is important that parents and other adults actively encourage the development of interests and learning different skills – such activities are interesting in their own right, but they also offer opportunities to meet and make friends.

Many young people with disabilities can lead very isolated lives, so access to a range of leisure facilities is important. Families may find that they are not well catered for in local leisure activities. However, some areas have after-school and holiday facilities that are accessible, either as integrated play facilities or as schemes that specifically cater for children and young people with disabilities.

Friends and parents

A different kind of relationship

Friendships in adolescence are very important. Young people in the early years of secondary school have close friends. Groups of friends can form stable cliques – not necessarily rejecting others, but supportive of each other. Young people tend to socialise in groups until such time as individuals start to pair off. (More on partnerships from page 133.) Friends are not necessarily lost once partnerships are formed but available time has to be shared.

Friends probably spend more time talking to each other than any other people in their circle, girls especially. This time with peers can be very important because, unlike relationships with parents – however good these are – friendships are conducted between equals in age and experience. Friendship time gives opportunities to practise many of the aspects of relationships that will be important in adult life and with partners.

Being part of a group of friends and spending time together can be a support to young people as they make the move from child to adult. However approachable and supportive their parents may be, young people also need close friendships – the two sources offer different kinds of support. For example:

- Children and young people will have conversations with friends that do not seem appropriate to have with parents. This does not necessarily mean that friends talk over forbidden topics; it is much more often the case that they chat about subjects they know will not interest their parents – at least not discussed at such length.
- With friends, they are also free to make the kind of offhand comments – perhaps about teachers or other adults – and giggle over the kind of jokes, that tend to make adults frown with disapproval.
- Children also point out that, 'You can muck about with friends' in a way that you cannot even with lively parents; it is not the same.
- Children and young people will also sometimes say that they might not mention something to parents if they might overreact and want to take some action when the situation is best left alone.

Generally, most young people think of their relationships with friends as separate and different from their relationships with their parents. This outlook is summed up well by the quotations on page 85.

Can adults help children with friendships?

Parents, teachers or club workers can neither make friends for children, nor push together two children or young people who have little in common. However, children are helped by parents whose family life encourages social skills that make finding and holding on to friends that much more likely. Other adults in children's lives may also be able to encourage positive approaches, as well as providing a good model by their own behaviour.

All the following appear to help children to make friendly contact and to have sustained friendships. The points have emerged in studies of children who have difficulty making friends, as well as those who find the process easier.

- The ability to listen to others as well as to talk.
- A willingness to support and encourage other children, as well as to accept encouragement in one's own turn.
- Avoiding an excessively critical approach to fellow children.
- Avoiding an aggressive or disruptive approach to the activities of other children.
- A sense of security and confidence in oneself, which does not require finding fault in others to sustain self-esteem.

Parents can help by making it easy, rather than difficult, for children and young people to bring their friends home. For children this tends to include a willingness to have several friends playing in the home and to tolerate the mild to more major disruption that this can bring. Daytime visits may develop into the occasional sleep-over for a few friends. A generous line on snacks and drinks and a welcoming approach to friends will be more likely to ensure that young people do bring their friends back to the home. With this sort of approach, parents are more likely to have some sense of what their young people are doing, as well as knowing whom to contact if young people are late home.

All of the above can be completely consistent with expecting visitors to any home to follow the house rules – preferably explained or shown by the children or young people who belong in the home.

The influence of friends

Children and young people are influenced by their friends – in their opinions, choice of clothes and how they want to spend their leisure time. Parents can become concerned if they feel a son or daughter is being unduly persuaded away from what the parent feels are proper values and behaviour. They worry about their children getting in with a 'bad' crowd, and the extent to which they will be able to stand up against pressures to conform to what this group of friends believes to be important. There is probably a limit to how far parents can succeed in shifting their child's allegiances and outright banning of any contact can often rebound. Perhaps what is most important is that parents:

make a genuine attempt to get to know their children's friends and make them welcome at home;

- keep good communication with their children and avoid full-scale criticism of their friends. A useful point to keep in mind is that parents rarely appreciate criticism from children about their own adult friends;
- are ready to spend time with children and young people when they want it and in the way that they would prefer;
- are ready to offer support if children are trying to break away from a crowd with whom they no longer want to associate.

Undoubtedly some groups of friends do encourage each other towards less wise behaviour. However, it is important not to confuse the workings of small friendship groups with the wilder excesses of large crowds. Studies of friendships in childhood and young adulthood suggest that friends sometimes pull each other out of trouble, rather than into it. The less excited members of a group do sometimes calm down a situation, or form a subgroup that supports each other in walking away. Young people with close relationships with their parents seem to be less vulnerable to pressures from friends to become involved in reprehensible activities.

Viewpoint

A young man in his early twenties reflected back over the more turbulent years of his adolescence.

'It's true that I certainly didn't behave well all the time. But it mattered a lot to me what my Dad thought. I was running with a mixed bunch of people – some of them were definitely ready to go over the line, do things that were against the law. Several times it was the thought of how disappointed my Dad would be that held me back. In the end several of us wanted out of that crowd and we pulled off together. We're still good friends now. The final straw was when one of the others had wanted us to give him an alibi for when he'd been housebreaking and we said, "No way!"'

Parents need to value a good relationship with their sons and daughters, while accepting that good friends will begin to dominate children and young people's social life. Families usually have to make some compromises over time spent together, the obligations of family gatherings and clashes in the respective social calendars of different members of the household.

13. Partnerships

Forming serious attachments

Young people tend to spend time as individuals with friends within groups until they start to form pairs. Couples do not necessarily then follow a social life completely separate from their friendship group, but may have some time that is exclusive to the two of them.

The situation for many young people in Britain now is that they are likely to have a series of couple relationships before they form a longer-lasting attachment, which may or may not last for their adult life. Young people usually face a situation in which early marriage is discouraged – few people have much positive to say about 'teenage marriages' – and where they are expected to choose their own partner. The pattern of relationships tends to be what has been described as a kind of 'serial monogamy' without marriage.

Families and young people's partnerships

When young people in mid- to late-adolescence start having serious, longer term relationships, their families have adjustments to make and some new concerns emerge:

- A serious relationship is evidence that their son or daughter has taken yet another step in the process of growing up and has allegiances outside the family. Some parents find this adjustment difficult.
- Parents may be pleased with the stability, so long as they like or can tolerate the partner. However, they feel there is another relationship within the family relations to handle.
- Parents also tend to start worrying because of concerns about whether there is a sexual element in the relationship, and the risk of unwanted pregnancy. Also, they may feel that the two young people are getting 'too serious' and closing down on their options too soon.
- Parents are also on the outside looking in on the relationship and hoping that, if and when a break up happens, their son or daughter will not be badly hurt.

When young people attend coeducational schools, the staff and fellow pupils will have views about appropriate and inappropriate expressions of affection between couples in school public life.

Any young people whose partnership crosses a cultural, religious or ethnic group divide can find their personal relationship apparently becoming the public property of many other people, including their respective families. The young people at the centre of these different kinds of 'mixed' partnerships may, themselves, be focusing solely on the individuality of their partners. Not all families, by any means, are resistant to their young people's wishes. But when families are opposed, young people can be faced with some very difficult decisions.

Religious faith and partnerships

Britain includes a wide range of different cultures and religious beliefs. Adults hold different views about the appropriateness of young people forming serious attachments which do not necessarily lead to marriage. This is not a dilemma restricted to any single world faith. Families with strongly-held Christian, Muslim, Hindu or Jewish beliefs can be seriously concerned about the moral behaviour of their young people. Groups such as Jehovah's Witnesses are equally concerned and prefer to take an uncompromising line against pre- and extra-marital sex, supporting their views with detailed reference to the scriptures.

Families with strong religious convictions against pre-marital sex tend to be especially concerned when young people form serious attachments before an age when marriage is likely to be a realistic option. Partnerships will involve sexual attraction, although not necessarily full sexual behaviour. However, parents with strong views are concerned about the temptations of a slippery slope of sexual attraction. Families with daughters can be anxious that a young woman's reputation will be shattered for ever, and that this will rebound on her relatives. Families whose faith is central to their lives may also be very concerned about inappropriate attachments, from their point of view, outside the family's faith.

Arranged marriages

The general pattern within Britain is to assume that young people will make their own choices over temporary partnerships or the decision to make a long-term commitment through marriage. Some cultures within Britain do not leave this important decision up to the young people themselves. There is a long tradition within many Asian and Oriental cultures, and within the stricter Jewish religious groups, that marriage is not only the relationship between two individuals but is also the uniting of two families. This awareness can be especially important when several generations share the family home and any new family member has to fit into the existing relationships.

Newspaper reports tend to focus on the potentially sensational aspect to arranged marriages – that of families who give their young people no choice and force a particular match upon them. Uncompromising authoritarian behaviour happens within every culture and it is not an accurate reflection of every arranged marriage. Many families involve the young people in the whole process, consulting them about possible partners and offering a choice of appropriate spouses.

Sexual awareness and behaviour

Many 11- and 12-year-olds are aware and interested in the relative attractiveness of other young people. They have opinions about what makes a physically attractive partner, as well as views on how their preferred partner should behave. As they move through puberty, many boys and girls are concerned that they should be considered attractive, even though practically they do not expect to form serious attachments for some years to come.

Young people's views

Lurid stories about sex, rather like drugs, sell newspapers and make lively television programmes. It can sometimes be hard for adults, especially worried parents, to feel reassured that their young people will not be swept along in an irresponsible way. Yet logic would suggest that sensational sex scandals are sensational largely because they are unusual.

It can be difficult to assess any surveys of sexual behaviour in a reliable way since they depend on people's reporting of their own actions and outlook. Replies to surveys are not always honest but the difficulty is in estimating whether young people, or anyone else replying, is over- or understating their level of sexual activity. (Readers can find reviews of the research in Moore and Rosenthal, 1993.)

Pre-marital sex is certainly not new, although the general outlook of young people seems to have changed in some ways when compared to that of previous generations.

- Young people seem to be more open about talking about sex or sexual issues than previous generations. Some, of course, may still be self-conscious, embarrassed or less knowledgeable than their language would suggest.
- Young people of the current generation seem to encounter ever more media pressure – more than their parents' generation – to judge themselves on physical attractiveness and clothes style from late childhood onwards.
- Young people are likely to view sexual behaviour as a private

matter – their own business and that of their partner – rather than being in the domain of public morality or their parents' business.

- The everyday reality for young people is less sensational than public image. The current generation of young people is far more discriminating in their sexual behaviour than some would believe. And previous generations were not the moral paragons of common myth!

Differences between young women and young men

Many, although not all, young people view sex as happening within a stable and lasting relationship. Different outlooks may be held by young men and women, in that the latter are more likely to regard sex within a relationship as proof of its stability, whereas young men do not necessarily look that far ahead. Young men seem more likely to view sexual activity as a proof of maturity and a way to establish social status. This outlook leads to the concern of some young women that they are talked about within the male friendship group.

Young people, and some older children who express opinions in this area, are aware that a double standard still operates for the behaviour of males and females. Sexual activity on the part of a young man is still far more likely to be regarded as acceptable, as evidence that he is 'a bit of lad'; in contrast, a sexually active young women risks being dismissed as a 'slag'. While taking a realistic view about the double standard, young women express their anger and irritation at its unfairness.

Continuing health conditions and disabilities

Young people are often very concerned about the beginnings of important relationships and the potential development of the physical side. Young people with a continuing health condition can experience an extra onslaught on their self-confidence. Many will wonder whether to tell a new partner about their health, especially if they have not been very open with friends. They are not only worrying about how far to go in a physical sense at what point in the relationship; they can also be racked over, 'What's he going to think when he realises how bad my eczema is?' or 'Suppose I go into a fit when we are out together. She'll dump me for sure.'

Young people with a continuing health condition often have new questions to ask as they become seriously involved in partnerships. Young men and women need reliable information, given in such a way that they are not embarrassed and feel able to ask for more. The booklet issued by the organisation Epilepsy and the Young Adult (1994) is a good example of what is needed. The booklet includes reassuring advice that sexual excitement will not trigger fits and practical information about contraceptive pills and epilepsy medication.

Young people with physical disabilities will be experiencing the same range of feelings as those who do not have to contend with disability in their everyday lives. Of course, the partners of young people with disabilities are not necessarily disabled themselves. At the same time as experiencing all the other adjustments of getting to know someone really well, the partners may be finding out about the difficulties of access for people with disabilities, or dealing with the thoughtlessness of other people.

When young people have serious learning disabilities, parents and other carers will be concerned that the young people themselves have some understanding of appropriate behaviour with the opposite sex and the practicalities of a safe physical relationship, without unexpected pregnancy.

Young people who are gay, lesbian or bisexual

There has undoubtedly been a great deal of rhetoric unleashed about sexual orientation. Reliable information is harder to find, but the indications are that the overall majority of young people and adults are heterosexual. The previously quoted proportion of up to one in ten of adults' being homosexual or bisexual has been largely discredited. However, even a much smaller proportion of the adult population would still give a substantial total number of men and women who are either bisexual or definitely attracted only to their own sex.

Most of the available studies are of adults, sure of their homosexual or bisexual orientation, who reflect back on their adolescent years. Some young people seem to spend a number of years uncertain about their sexual orientation, yet others will say later that they had no doubt about their sexuality from puberty onwards. Apart from the usual difficulties of making and sustaining important couple relationships, gay young men and lesbians are also likely to be dealing with other problems and pressures.

- Their awareness of social pressure from friends and family, pushing them towards attempts at heterosexuality.
- Discomfort or disapproval from family or friends. Some parents are especially saddened by the loss of the prospect of grandchildren.
- Parents and others may disapprove on moral grounds. The major world religious faiths take an uncompromising and negative attitude towards active homosexuality.
- The practical issues of finding a partner when many pressures will be against honesty over a non-heterosexual orientation.
- The legal situation on age of consent for same-sex partners (see page 149).

The factors that precipitate a young person towards homosexuality are far from clear, but it does seem that the ground is laid, by a combination of biological and social factors, from an early age. Attempts to argue young people out of their preferred sexual orientation, or to 'cure' them, are most likely to lead to a rift between the adults and young person.

Some parents, and other concerned adults, may find it difficult to accept homosexuality in young people or may be convinced that it is a phase from which the young person will emerge in time. Undoubtedly some young people, in the earlier years of adolescence, can have very intense feelings towards a friend of the same sex. They seem able to distinguish intense friendship from sexual attraction, although some may feel unsure for a while. A further confusing factor seems to enter when young people are living in single-sex, enclosed environments such as boarding schools. Strong sexual feelings may join with restricted availability to lead to homosexual encounters, which are not later repeated.

The law and sexuality

Sexual behaviour

The legal framework is part of the message to young people about when they are deemed mature enough to be allowed, legally, to take certain actions. However, it is striking that, even within Europe, there is no consistency over the ages.

In England, Wales and Scotland young people have to be 16 years of age to engage, legally, in heterosexual sex, 18 years old if they are gay young men, but 16 if lesbians. However, the judgements are not the same elsewhere in Europe. For instance, in Northern Ireland the ages are 17, 18 and 17 years respectively. In France, the age of consent for any heterosexual, gay or lesbian sex is 15 years. In Germany, the judged mature age is 14 for heterosexual and lesbian sex and 18 for gay young men.

There will be historical reasons for the differences, but the basic point remains that, within the same continent, adults in positions of authority to make the laws of the land have come to different conclusions about the age of sufficient maturity for personal decisions about sexual relations.

Obtaining contraception

The legal situation is confused over making contraception available to young people, usually females, who are under the legal age of consent to sexual behaviour.

In 1969 the Family Law Reform Act established that young people could make their own medical decisions from 16 years of age. A young person can give agreement to medical or surgical decisions, without their parents' consent and the medical profession are required to respect the confidentiality of consultations with over 16-year-olds. However, it was left up to the judgement of individual doctors whether they offered contraceptive advice and treatment to young people under the age of 16 years. This principle was confirmed in 1980 by the Department of Health.

Victoria Gillick went to court to challenge the possibility that doctors could prescribe contraceptives to under-sixteens without parents' knowledge and consent. In 1985, the final judgment on the case was that doctors could offer such advice without infringing parental rights, so long as a girl aged under 16 had sufficient understanding to give her consent. This case established what has been called the Gillick principle. However, the legal position remains uncertain, because the principle has not become part of written law. Doctors and clinics are cautious about offering contraceptive advice to under-sixteens because their judgement of whether a girl was capable of making her own decision is open to challenge in court by parents who object.

Although contraception is a specific instance, the dilemma is part of the broader issue of the age at which young people are judged to be in charge of their own health and medical decisions. Dilemmas have arisen when parents have wanted a procedure such as the sterilisation of a young woman who has severe learning disabilities, judging that the operation is in her best interests.

Risk and sexual activity

Placing any moral or legal considerations on one side, adults remain concerned about young people's sexual behaviour if they feel unable to trust them to behave in a responsible or safe way.

Pregnancy

Whatever the final outcome from how the situation is handled, unexpected pregnancy is an event that changes the lives of young women, their families and, to a greater or lesser extent, the fathers of the babies.

Children and young people in state schools receive sex education as a specific topic and within the science lessons of their school curriculum, although parents may insist that their children do not attend the separate sex education lessons. Some parents are open in talking about sex and related issues with their children. This generation of young people has access to information and can purchase some forms of contraception over the counter from high street stores. Yet, pregnancies still happen – and at a time when they can be seriously disruptive to young people's lives and studies. There seem to be several reasons why rationality does not win out for some young couples:

- Some sexual experiences happen without any forward planning.
- Young people may show a reticence, shared by previous generations, in raising practical issues of contraception during times of passion.
- Some young men and young women still hold on to inaccurate beliefs, or convenient hopes, about ways in which you cannot

become pregnant. Included is the time-honoured hope that 'we won't get caught out'.

- Knowledge about pregnancy and contraception may encourage some young people towards caution. However, some young women become pregnant knowingly. If they have few qualifications and see little prospect of a job, they may see no point in postponing their wish for a baby. Some may look towards a baby as an individual all of their own, who will love them unreservedly.
- Some young people take risks partly because the prospect of a baby does not seem too difficult. They may have very unrealistic beliefs about how their current life could continue as it is, with the simple addition of a young baby.

Some schools build some level of preparation for parenthood into their programmes of personal and social education, which may also include the sex education which is not delivered through the science curriculum. Young people may not be interested in thinking and talking directly about their own future experience of parenthood – it seems a less immediate concern for them, in comparison to other issues. Young people can, however, be motivated to discuss family life, as they experience it now, and some – boys as well as girls – can become very interested in how babies and children develop and what they need. Teachers who run any courses of this type have to be careful since discussion about parenting immediately invites young people to reflect on their own families and childhood. This can open up private family matters or sometimes painful experiences.

Sexually transmitted diseases

Sex education programmes in schools cover sexually transmitted diseases, at least to some extent. It is very difficult to judge to what extent this information is affecting the sexual behaviour of young people.

Young people tend to have an optimism that they will not be affected or a conviction that the risk of sexually transmitted diseases will not be faced within their group – they are things that happen to other people. They are aware of AIDS, because of the high level of publicity, but do not necessarily believe that it is a genuine risk for them. The high profile of AIDS seems, to some extent, to have reduced awareness of other sexually transmitted diseases which, although not fatal, can seriously affect people's health before they are effectively treated, sometimes leaving permanent problems.

14. The experience of school

In Britain, though education is compulsory, school attendance itself is not mandatory. Some families choose to educate their children at home, in which case the local authority will want to be reassured that parents have a consistent plan for how they will support their children's learning. However, for the majority of families, education will mean school attendance by their children from the ages of five to 16 years, and for some young people, on to 18 years.

Attitudes towards school

Children and young people spend a considerable number of hours in total in school, whether this a state school or one from the independent sector. Their obligations to attend school and their study commitments are a major influence on how they can organise the rest of their life. School will be the source of some, although not all of their friendships and some of their positive feelings about school may arise from the social opportunities. In coeducational schools, school life may be the source of closer relationships that develop into partnerships.

Viewpoint

Having to attend school is seen by some young people as one of the strands that tie them into childhood. Although some older pupils in the school discussion groups mentioned, with satisfaction, that teachers treat them differently in later years, this does not always appear to be the case. Part of the decision to attend sixth form college rather than a sixth form within school seems to relate to a wish to break with the setting in which young people were perceived as children.

Older children and young people who described what growing up means for them, sometimes specifically mentioned that leaving school and finishing with all their exams would be a significant turning point.

It is worth recalling that compulsory education up to the age of 16 years is a relatively recent phenomenon. In the previous decades of schooling for all children, young people were permitted to leave school at ages which now are classified, at least partly, as within childhood. Prior to the 1970s' change in the school leaving age, 15-year-olds were able to leave. In the 1920s and 1930s, children who did not pass to go to the local county school were out in the world of work at 14 years of age – at the turn of the century, it was 13 years.

Over the same period that schools have been extending the age range of their pupils there has been an expansion in the expectations of what schools will achieve. As well as core skills of literacy and numeracy, schools are expected to deliver a broad education and to prepare children and young people for life and work in a society that is changing, sometimes in highly unpredictable ways.

These are ambitious aims and it is hardly surprising that a proportion of children and young people continue to attend schools under duress, having decided that schooling and the school ethos is not for them. Many schools have two distinct groups of pupils – those who are generally pro- and those who are anti-school. These pupils tend to form different subcultures in the school.

Positive views of school

The pupils who feel positively about school do not always like every subject or admire every teacher, but they do feel a commitment to the overall process of gaining an education. They feel it will be worth it in the end. These pupils have broadly accepted the value system of the

---

Viewpoint

Even children who are generally positive towards school will have their 'off days' and wish to unload complaints at home. Children and young people look to parents for time and some understanding. They do not appear to expect that parents will magically make everything all right, but do ask for a sympathetic hearing, focused on what has happened.

Ten- to 14-year-olds summed up what many children and young people wanted:

- 'They (parents) say, "In my day, people used to love school." They go on and on about how school was for them. They don't put themselves in our shoes.'
- 'My Dad says he didn't like school, but he still doesn't seem to understand what it's like for me.'
- 'I want sympathy from my parents if I complain about some of the teachers.'
- 'Perhaps you're nagging on about your day at school and they say, "I've had a hard day. You don't know the half of it!" And they go on about what's happened to them.'
- 'It doesn't help if parents go on about how when they were young and how much homework they had.'

school, although they may well complain about details of school discipline. They are prepared to work hard and their motivation is sustained by satisfaction in school study, interest in most of what they are learning and a pleasure in the symbols of good work, such as high marks and the pleasure of teachers and parents.

Negative outlooks on schools

The pupils who are hostile or indifferent to schooling and its values tend to play the system for a sense of personal control and entertainment. They develop sometimes quite sophisticated patterns for baiting teachers, challenging authority over any school rules or codes like uniform, and in selectively avoiding classes or truanting entirely. Encouraging and cajoling these children and young people back into the school system can be very difficult. Teachers may have labelled them as troublesome and the pupils themselves have lost the habit of concentration and no longer look for interest in any school subject.

Once children and young people have developed negative attitudes to school, it can be hard to justify the school experience subject by subject. There is no simple link to be made for a young person between asking them to take seriously the study of the crusades or the development of modern Japan and what may or may not be of direct practical use for them in later life. In times of high unemployment, especially in areas particularly badly affected, neither teachers nor parents can promise jobs as a result of hard work and qualifications.

Effective schools

Even well-motivated pupils will not find every subject interesting and much will depend on the quality of teaching. Schools vary on a number of characteristics. However, effective schools are distinguished by the behaviour and beliefs of the staff. In the more effective schools:

- Teaching staff are convinced that all pupils are capable of learning.
- Staff have high expectations of their pupils. Expecting a lot can also be compatible with realistic expectations for different pupils.
- Staff spend more time in interaction with pupils.
- Teachers make more effort to reward and acknowledge pupils' work.
- Staff have friendlier classrooms. A friendly classroom can exist alongside clear ground rules for the class.
- Children and young people are consulted on school policy and have a forum, such as school councils, in which to voice opinions. The consultation only works well when pupils see some results from their suggestions.

Teachers need to expect the most from children and young people, and let them know what and how they have achieved – and not just in

academic terms. Consistent encouragement of this kind is just as important in schools as buying the latest computer software or how many books they have. Indeed, resources alone cannot do the work in schools. What matters is how well the resources are integrated by teachers into the pattern of instruction in lessons.

Diversity in the school population

Schools have to be responsive to the needs of all their pupils. All schools will have some diversity among their pupils, but some can have a wide variety – in terms of ethnic group, cultural background and religious belief.

All pupils from minority ethnic groups need to see an active respect for their culture and individuality reflected in school life as well as in the curriculum. Schools have a responsibility to investigate whether pupils of any ethnic or social group are disproportionately represented in lower ability streams or school disciplinary procedures. The reasons are unlikely to be straightforward, but the explanation cannot be that an entire subgroup of pupils lacks ability or is irretrievably badly behaved.

Muslim families in Britain can face particular issues over religion and school life. The families do not have the option of sending their children to specifically Muslim state schools unlike, for instance, Catholic families. Families may want schools to cater for their family diet, allow girls and young women to cover their heads and legs and make provision for regular daily prayer. All these issues are part of their young people's cultural and religious identity. Not all Muslim families will make these requests since, as with every major world faith, there is considerable variety within Islamic practice. Some schools find an acceptable approach to such requests, for example, asking that head coverings are in the school colours and allowing all pupils to wear trousers should they wish. Other schools have, in the past, been unwilling to make any compromises.

Children with disabilities

Children with physical, sensory or learning disabilities may attend mainstream schools or special units within schools, or they may be catered for by a separate educational provision. The pattern of provision varies in different parts of the country, but there has been an increase in the number of children who have a place within mainstream schools.

Children with disabilities will always need specific support appropriate to their individual needs. In mainstream primary and secondary schools the help may be provided through additional teaching time, perhaps with a specialist teacher. Special equipment can be a help for some children, for instance those with communication difficulties.

A non-teaching assistant (NTA) may provide regular help to one or more children in a class. When individual helpers are outgoing and pleasant with other pupils in the class, they can be seen as a genuine asset to the group, although it is fully understood that their prime responsibility is to the pupil with disabilities.

Relationships between children

Children or young people within the school may be a genuine help to pupils with disabilities, so long as they have some guidance on the best way to offer support. However, all pupils have responsibilities of their own and fellow students should not be seen as the main strand of support.

Schools sometimes have to handle complex issues that arise when special facilities or privileges appear to be available only to the pupils with disabilities. Children and young people are very sharp over the matter of fairness and they may feel they have been short-changed – even when staff are sure that they have explained carefully why certain pupils are excused particular lessons or that separate funding has paid for the special unit's equipment.

For many children and young people the key issue can be that pupils with disabilities have to follow the same codes of behaviour as everyone else and are not 'allowed to get away with things'. One group of 12-year-olds (in the school discussions undertaken for this book) became very heated about the cavalier driving of a few pupils in wheelchairs through the school corridors. In one sense, the young people's focus on fairness was consistent with the approach of treating children with disabilities as, first and foremost, children.

The relationship with teachers

During the 1980s and 1990s the curriculum and teaching methods of state primary and secondary schools have been significantly revised. (For more details see, for instance, J. and L. Lindon, 1995. Children and young people need to be offered a full and well-taught curriculum, but their school experience and outlook is still highly influenced by the working relationships they build with teachers and those between their parents and the school staff.

Children and young people

Children in primary school are most likely to have a class teacher who will take most subjects with them and a small number of other teachers who have specialist skills, for instance, in dance or music. For primary school children their relationships with support staff can also be important in how they view school. Helpers, who are not teachers, may well be the adults supervising playground times and therefore the first port of call for children who are bored or who are experiencing troubles with other children.

Secondary school pupils have to manage a network of relationships with many staff – their form teacher or group tutor and probably as many other teachers as subjects they are taking. A form teacher may get to know pupils fairly well, especially in schools where this teacher travels through from Year 7 to the end of school life with the group of pupils. However, other teachers will not get to know individual pupils very well and pupils are unlikely to feel that they have a close relationship with other than a few teachers at most.

Children and young people develop clear likes and dislikes, which they can usually explain in terms that make logical sense to them, although the importance they place on some issues may be disputed by adults. In general pupils tend to seek the following:

- *Teachers who are able to keep control over the class*
  Less confident or firm teachers may give more scope for playing about, but are not respected. Pupils who wish to work can become very irritated by teachers who do not maintain the calm they need in order to concentrate or who fail to curb disruptive behaviour from other pupils.
- *Teaching staff should behave in a reasonably predictable and fair way*
  Children and young people want to know where they are with a teacher. It can be unsettling to try to relate to a teacher who sometimes jokes about and then at other times does not.

- *Teachers should be consistent in their application of any school rules and guidelines*
  For instance, once there is a definite homework timetable, pupils are critical of teachers who give homework on the 'wrong' night. Schools who develop codes of conduct for their pupils will find that children and young people are scathing about teachers who do not follow rules that should, in pupils' views, be equally applicable to them – for example, turning up on time for lessons or promptly marking homework that pupils have given in promptly.
- *Teachers should be fair in their treatment of individuals*
  Neither children nor young people appreciate teachers who have obvious favourites within a class, and the favoured pupil may also find that the discomfort of being singled out far outweighs any pleasure felt.

Parents

This generation of parents is experiencing perhaps the greatest openness of schools to parents. Apart from the genuine wish on the part of some heads and their staff to have close working relationships with parents, the legislation supporting the National Curriculum obliges schools to keep parents informed about the progress of their children.

Although parents' physical access to schools is considerably easier than it was 30 years ago, a wide range of attitudes towards parents is still held by teachers. Parents may be viewed as:

- *Partners* – who are working together with teachers, although in different ways, to help children to learn.
- *Customers* – of the educational service, who have a right to expect high standards in the service and to contribute to policy decisions that will affect the direction that the school takes.
- *Clients* – who have problems or difficulties for which they are seeking help from the school.
- *Problems* – whose access to the school and influence on their children is best restricted. Parents may be regarded by teachers as problems because they are judged to be making an unreasonable fuss about an issue, or because they are believed to be the cause of their child's learning or behavioural difficulties.

There are many examples from schools of cooperative ventures between teachers and parents. However, even in schools attempting to pursue an active partnership with parents, the relationship can become frosty when either party is judged to be overstepping the boundaries of their role. Teachers may not welcome meetings in which parents express serious concerns about teaching methods or standards. Parents, on the other hand, do not usually appreciate being told how to behave with their child within family life.

To think about

Teachers and parents may feel an equal level of concern about children and young people but their roles are not the same. Teachers have to spread their concern around a large number of children, whereas caring parents have, as their proper focal point, their own sons and daughters.

The two perspectives can lead to disagreements or misunderstandings, but they are not incompatible in a partnership between home and school if all the adults involved are prepared to expend some effort.

Studies of the relationship between parents and schools have regularly confirmed that the majority of parents are concerned about their children and young people, and wish to support them in their school experience. They wish to know what is happening and to be consulted about anything of importance for their own child. Additionally, some parents want practical advice on how to help their children with particular problems they are experiencing in study generally or in specific subjects.

Misunderstandings can arise when schools have a narrow definition of partnership with parents and expect parents to fit in with the timing and types of meetings devised mainly by teachers. Some parents are very pleased to develop their social life through fund-raising activities for the school, or to help the school, but others do not wish for this kind of relationship. It is important that teachers do not judge parent commitment largely from attendance at specific kinds of functions. In the same way, parents have to allow for the reality that teachers have obligations to other children and families and cannot be expected to drop everything for one parent's convenience.

Parents may prefer to build their relationships with schools through

To think about

The educational process, and teachers who deliver it, have a status and aura of professionalism, despite the disagreements and disruption of recent years. Because they are viewed as experts, teachers have been increasingly expected to train children and young people in broad life skills that could well be regarded as the role of parents – sex education and parenting skills, road safety, general social skills, a sense of responsibility to others, a sense of right and wrong. Some parents, in their turn, have begun to doubt their own ability to do their part in helping their children to grow up, because, 'surely teachers know better what to do – they are trained.'

It is well worth considering, when faced with any claim that 'the schools should be doing this', to what extent the skills or knowledge should be imparted by children's own parents or in a more effective partnership between home and school.

informal contact rather than more formal meetings. During the primary school years, when children are taken to school, there may be many more opportunities for brief conversations. This kind of informal contact reduces as children take themselves to school and with the different arrangements at secondary school. Meetings arranged to talk about children or young people can still offer an opportunity to talk in a relaxed way about progress and any problems. However, much depends on the approach taken by teachers, on whose territory these meetings happen.

School work and study

The support of parents

Generally speaking, children and young people who look positively on school have parents who support them and are ready to help them in any way possible. This is not an exact relationship; few, if any, patterns involving people are this certain. Some children and young people progress well at school with very little positive support and some who have full back-up from their parents nevertheless take a serious dislike to school and study.

In the end, parents cannot do the work for their children and young people, but their valuable contribution is to offer the following:

- A positive attitude towards school, study and teachers.
- The willingness to find out what is going on at school and to attend meetings.
- Time and energy to help children and young people with the work they bring home and in the run up towards tests and exams.
- A parent's backing and presence, when necessary, to resolve any serious or persistent problems that children or young people have during their years at school.

Likes and dislikes in subjects

Children and young people are unlikely to enjoy all subjects equally and, unless they are getting effective help, children generally tend to dislike the subjects with which they are struggling.

In primary school, a form teacher will teach most of the school subjects, but in secondary school, students will have subject teachers. It can be important that children develop a liking for school and for school subjects that is independent of liking or disliking individual teachers. Teachers do matter and the risk posed by a poor quality primary school teacher is that he or she may put a child off school as a whole, as well as blocking their progress for the time they are together. The link between specific subjects and teachers can become more problematic when young people are at secondary school. Liking the teacher is an advantage and can be a support in a subject that does not come easily. But, if the teacher becomes too closely associated with a subject, then a later – disliked – teacher may sabotage much of the earlier work.

Viewpoint

One father described the meeting he had attended for his son concerning the end of Year 9 options and the choices that the pupils had to make ready for the GCSE years:

'The careers teacher took some time to go through how the boys could make choices and she stressed about not depending on who you thought would be teaching the subject. From the looks on some of the boys' faces and the muttered comments I could see that, for them, teachers could get very tied into subject choices.'

Help with homework

Children and young people look towards their parents for some help in the work that they bring home. In primary school this tends to be learning spellings or times tables and finishing off work that children did not complete in class time. Secondary school pupils have set homework and the amount grows as they pass through the school. Offering help and support requires a commitment of time and energy from parents.

Views of children and young people

The comments frequently made by children and young people in the schools' discussion groups can be summarised as follows:

- Ideally, it's nice to be given the answers, but children and young people appreciate that, if parents help you to work out the answers yourself, then you know what to do next time.
- When children and young people have to commit knowledge to memory, they appreciate help in writing things out and being tested – but only when they are ready.
- It is better for parents to ask if children and young people want help, or to wait until help is requested, rather than to insist on helping.
- Some children and young people are sensitive to their parents' feelings and feel awkward about turning down help that they really do not want – or not at this time.
- Sometimes children are so confused, they just want things explained. This can become progressively difficult for parents to manage, unless they have a flair for a particular subject.
- Parents need to accept that their answers may sometimes be

wrong and to check, or admit that they do not know or cannot remember.

- Parents need to recall that, in the end, the homework belongs to their son or daughter. Children and young people will have their own way of doing things, of thinking, and it is unlikely to be helpful for parents to insist. Projects in the end belong to the child or young person, however interested a parent has become in helping in the search for information.

- It is no shame for parents to admit that they cannot help. As the secondary school years pass by, young people's friends or older brothers and sisters may be better placed to help.

- Children and young people do not want to be nagged over their homework. But some admit that they need to be pushed, although they are not keen. Parents probably cannot win on this one.

- Young people want appreciation and recognition of just how hard they have to work for GCSEs and then for A levels, GNVQs or other further qualifications. Parents are less likely to be able to help in the detail, but they can support by understanding the weight of study and being flexible over domestic issues.

Children's views of their ability

Children and young people need an optimistic outlook on their ability that does not, unrealistically, overestimate what they can do. Probably all children compare themselves with others and even able children can feel daunted by classmates who have an outstanding ability in a subject.

Children and young people have to come to terms with the reality that achieving a personal best within schoolwork needs a combination of ability and hard work. Children sometimes seem to undervalue hard work, feeling that success somehow does not count for as much if it was reached with a struggle. They point to friends who are 'good at science', but 'I find it so hard'. A child with a flair for languages or for maths may well understand an idea more quickly or genuinely need less practice before confidently using a new technique.

Children and young people can follow two different patterns in making sense of what they manage with relative ease and what is experienced as more difficult.

1. Explaining success as being down to hard work in class or homework, and failure to lack of ability in the subject.
2. Explaining success as emerging out of ability in this subject, and failure to lack of effort in study.

The first approach entails the risk that children or young people will not value their success because being 'good at a subject' is what counts. There is also the built-in risk that children with this approach will give up on some subjects which are difficult for them because, since they are 'no good at maths', there is no point in making the effort. Children and young people with the second approach may emerge from relative failure with their self-confidence more intact, since they can explain it away by thinking, 'I could have done better if I'd tried harder.' The problem for parents and the young people themselves is then one of motivation to make more effort.

Studies of the views of girls and boys have shown some average differences between the sexes. Girls seem more likely to follow the first approach and boys the second approach (see page 59.)

Children and young people need a blend of outlooks:

- A pleasure when they have talent or absorbing interest in a subject.
- The motivation to put in the effort to realise their potential.
- The recognition that everyone has to work at the school subjects, even those who have outstanding ability. The striking point about children who are gifted – in maths, science, music, physical skills – is the tremendous amount of time and practice they have put in.

Troubles with other children

It is very unlikely that any child will pass through the years of schooling without encountering some sort of trouble with other children. Some of these difficulties are mild and children manage to sort matters out to their own satisfaction. Other situations are more complex and the problems more persistent.

Bullying

In recent years there has been considerably more recognition of the problems that children and young people experience from their interaction with each other. The kind of persistent baiting or attacking of another child that can be described as bullying is not a new phenomenon. Adults often have sharp memories of childhood difficulties brought about by their experience of being bullied, or of what another child suffered over a period of time. What has changed is that adults responsible for children are now far less likely to dismiss bullying as 'just part of childhood'. There is more recognition that bullying causes immense distress, and that adults have a responsibility to help.

What is bullying?

Children will experience some temporary troubles or disagreements with other children, even between good friends. Bullying is a more sustained and unjustified cruelty directed at another child. This type of aggressive behaviour is not always physical, although some children are attacked or intimidated by the threat of physical violence. Other children and young people can be terribly distressed by a persistent campaign of verbal bullying. Bullies may pick on almost anything – size, style of clothes, a child's family, physical appearance, ethnic group, religion. Some bullying by groups or individuals may have sexual overtones. Other patterns of bullying are organised around intimidating other children into handing over money or possessions.

Bullying is not a pattern restricted to childhood or to schools. Many adults will say that bullying happens in the workplace, sometimes to a high level. Children or young people bully for much the same basic reasons that adults torment others. They want and enjoy the feeling of power over others and will continue until they are stopped and/or find another way to feel confident and important in their own lives.

Children tend to get involved in bullying others through slightly different routes:

- Some children have been so indulged that they see no reason why they cannot have whatever they want.
- Some children or young people who bully were, in the past, on the receiving end of bullying from others. In a sense, they are getting their own back now that they are bigger, or feel stronger, or have a group of friends to support their actions.
- Some children are pulled in because they are part of a group that bullies others and they cannot see how to remove themselves from the bullying without losing their friends.

There is no subgrouping of children or young people of whom anyone could say, with confidence, 'They will never bully'. Boys tend to take the more physical routes but some girls will also use at least the threat of physical attack. On average, girls who bully are more likely to use words to hurt and humiliate. But some boys, who have caused immense distress, have carried out a sustained campaign of insults and innuendo against other children. Children from minority ethnic groups can be on the receiving end of bullying that is racist in intention and result. Yet, in schools with a mixed ethnic population, these children may well be active in a pattern of bullying others on a range of non-racial grounds.

A whole-school approach

Bullying cannot be tackled unless schools admit that it exists and establish a whole-school policy on behaviour, including bullying. Such a policy will only work well if all the school staff are fully committed and there is a close link between school and home. No school has any excuse for not having a policy since there is a wealth of practical information and guidance now available. (See, for example, Elliott, 1991.)

Some schools, often in partnership with parents, have taken an approach to bullying that is integrated with the school's pastoral system or personal and social education curriculum. There has then been a broad-based attempt to influence how children and young people deal with their own worries and their personal wish for a sense of confidence, and how they relate to others in a large organisation such as a school.

Specific approaches to instances of bullying have focused not only on the particular incident but also on working with the children or young people who bully, in order to prevent them continuing in this way. Some schools have set up programmes that involve pupils, for example, through such initiatives as 'bully courts' or systems to enable pupils to talk with other pupils initially, rather than having to approach teachers. Teachers and playground support staff need to be vigilant and to take children's troubles seriously. A significant part of trying to help children tends to be the school guideline that they should tell teachers about bullying – and should definitely take this approach rather than trying to deal with their problems themselves by fighting.

Children's perspective

Telling is a sound idea that, as children explain, is less straightforward in practice. A group of ten- and 11-year-olds made the following points from their viewpoint:

- 'Sometimes you tell and nothing happens, or the helper just says, "Ignore them". Or they think you're making a fuss about nothing.'
- 'If you tell, then sometimes the teachers aren't very discreet about helping you out.'
- 'They don't seem to realise that you don't want to tell because you get called "chicken" or you get threatened by the other child, or their friends.'
- 'It's not easy to tell and sometimes you think, "Why can't they see that I'm having all this trouble, isn't it obvious?"'

None of these realistic concerns expressed by children mean that trying to create a 'telling' school is a bad idea. The children's perspective is a timely reminder that school and playground life is complicated and adults neither see nor understand everything that goes on. Perhaps the adult perspective will always be different; their responsibilities are different.

Teachers usually ask that children do not hit back, but come and tell instead, and often prefer that children do not answer rude taunts and so on with verbal insults. However, as children and young people point out – and sometimes their parents too – unless teachers can guarantee to stop the physical or verbal attacks, they cannot really expect children who wish to behave well to deny themselves these forms of self defence.

Transitions

The many changes

School experience for children and young people is one of a series of changes. Within primary school, children have different teachers over the years, they have to get used to different classrooms as their base and may also move into different sections of the playground as they get older. Along with these changes, children experience the shifting expectations of teachers as they get older within the school. Ten- and 11-year-olds appreciate being given more responsibility in their position at the top end of primary school.

In state schools most children make the transition to the secondary stage at the age of 11 years, at the end of Year 6, although a few move on at the end of Year 5. Children in the independent sector move to the next stage at 13 years of age. Children are best involved in the choice of secondary school, where there is more than one possible school. However, the final decision may well have to made by parents who are weighing up educational issues, along with their child's preference and an important element of 'gut feel' about a school.

The move into secondary school

Eleven-year-olds may well be excited about moving on to secondary school, since it is another step in growing up. However, the transition has its difficult aspects, and some of them can foresee the adjustments that they will have to make. Pupils in their Year 7 point to the following issues that they faced:

- From being the eldest and biggest at primary school, they start all over again at what feels like the bottom of the pile – the youngest and littlest.
- Children have to get used to homework. They feel there's a lot of it and it can be hard to fit it in with other things they want to do. Getting organised after school and weekends requires new skills and the motivation to get down to work.
- Most secondary schools are considerably bigger than primary schools and children have to get used to finding their way around. Most get lost at some time within the first couple of weeks, before they get the area mapped out in their heads.
- There are many other children to get to know and sometimes children do not have any friends from their old school in their new class. Some may have gone to a school that few, if any, of their primary school friends are now attending. New status systems start to develop in the group and some children may face problems with other children that take time to resolve.
- With as many teachers as subjects and a form teacher, children

have to get to know a lot of new – and quite important – adults. They are all a bit different in their ways.

- Most children and their parents remark on how tired the Year 7 pupils are, especially in the first couple of terms. This exhaustion may be partly an earlier start to the day and perhaps a longer journey. However, the physical and mental exhaustion seems also to come from all the moving about within the school that is part of the timetable. Few schools now have desks and, even with lockers, children carry heavy bags around during the day and to and from home.
- Children often remark that there are so many things to remember – homework, books, the right kit for the right days – and that this can be a strain, since teachers expect them not to forget.

Good secondary schools make a lot of effort to welcome the new Year 7 intake and to ease them into the work. Some schools organise full or half day visits in the preceding summer term, a start for the Year 7 pupils before the rest of the school in the autumn term and a programme of familiarisation with the school during the first few days.

Parents can help tremendously by recognising the changes that the boys and girls have to manage, and supporting them with time and attention to hear how everything is going. Listening to complaints about different aspects of the new school can be rather wearing for parents. But it is an important way to help, and the only way to get some perspective on which are the temporary problems that will fade away and which are the more persistent ones that may need further help.

Leaving school

Children and young people who look ahead to leaving school see this step as a major move out of childhood into a more adult life. They may be leaving for further study, in which case there is a sense of moving on to a more mature stage in their life, although they are still financially dependent on their family. Young people who are not involved in any kind of further study or training are attempting to make the move into the world of work.

The feelings of young people

Leaving school can be an experience that affects young people in different ways. For many school leavers, the leaving itself is linked with a sense of relief that exams are finally over. The results are yet to come, but the former pupils have emerged from a long tunnel in which their lives had to revolve around study, the completion of projects and the actual sit-down exams. Various kinds of celebrations in school or elsewhere often follow.

Those who have gained satisfaction, on balance, from their years in school may feel some regrets which tinge the excitement of moving on. Young people who have felt positively about school as a whole may have gained self-confidence from their school work and involvement in school activities. They may also be aware, even if only faintly, that they will have to establish themselves again, whether in their place of further training or study, or in a job.

Some young people feel nothing but relief to have the school part of their life over. Some may in fact have been disengaged from school for some time, perhaps physically absent through truanting, or there in body but scarcely in mind. These young people may yet find a form of further training that is more to their taste, but their overwhelming feeling for now is that at last they are free of the restrictions of compulsory schooling.

The feelings of parents

Parents too can have mixed feelings. This stage in their son or daughter's life is overwhelming evidence that the young people are almost grown up. Parents may feel trepidation on behalf of their young people, knowing that colleges and other places of further training and study will not necessarily be easy options. Where unemployment is high or jobs are limited, parents may also be worried about how their young people will get a job and what they will do with their time if this proves very difficult. Those who have not managed to move their offspring into being more actively helpful in family life may be seriously concerned that they will have a young person on their hands who does little and brings in next to no money to help support the household.

Young people with disabilities

The shift to leaving school may be different for young people with physical or learning disabilities. Young people may find that, especially in times of unemployment, they have an even tougher time than friends as they search for a job. Young people who are moving on to some form of further education may have to organise themselves around different, or more complex, travelling arrangements. They may also have to set up new systems for the kind of support they will need to sustain and enable their studies.

Young people with multiple or complex disabilities may have a very limited choice for continuing education or vocational training. The statutory assessments cease when a young person leaves school. However, all young people with disabilities have to have what are called transition plans (under the Code of Practice of the Education Act 1993). Such plans should ensure that young people have an accurate and positive plan for their next stage. Young people may find the further education and training they want in a specialist residential college or in the further education college of their choice, so long as additional help is available. In reality, families can experience difficulties in making a transition to suitable post-school settings. They are also negotiating the transfer from children's services to those for adults.

15.   Young people and work

School and the preparation for work

The sole aim of all the years of compulsory schooling is not just to prepare young people for the job market. However, the link is increasingly expected to be reasonably close during secondary school between what young people do in school, the qualifications they gain and their consequent chances to get paid work.

Schools have been criticised in the past, sometimes harshly, for inadequate preparation of young people for the requirements of getting and holding a job. Many secondary schools have responded by more direct and comprehensive programmes of career advice, of issues such as good self-presentation in an interview, and work experience during Years 10 or 11 and, sometimes, Year 12. However, it is unrealistic to expect schools to do all the preparation of young people and even the most careful programmes, and gaining relevant qualifications, are no guarantee of a job in a changing economic climate.

Work experience

It is now common practice for secondary school students to be given one or more sessions of work experience. The aims are twofold:

1. To provide an accurate experience of work itself.
2. To give an opportunity for young people, who have a clear idea of what they would like to do, to get an understanding of what the job is really like in practice.

Schools will organise the placements for young people. But they have many pupils to place and are usually more than happy for young people to generate their own preferences for their particular work experience – even to organise it, with the help of their parents in making suitable contacts or writing letters.

Sometimes the work experience confirms that young people's first, or second, choices will suit them. However, it can be equally useful to discover that the job is nothing like they envisaged. Some young people find out that an absorbing interest may best be pursued during their leisure time, rather than as their job.

Some young people have only a very vague idea of what job they might prefer. The work experience can then give them a more accurate idea of what is expected of anyone in paid work. They are sometimes surprised, even shocked, to discover that workplaces have some very firm expectations with regard to behaviour, time-keeping, dress and so on.

The usefulness of the experience will depend on the quality of schools' contacts with potential work experience placements, and how carefully teachers monitor the pupils and gain feedback after the couple of weeks are complete. In addition, the value of the experience depends both on the young people themselves and on the organisation where they spend their time – successful placements involve some effort on the part of the host organisation to show young people the different aspects to the work.

Young people's perspective

The opinions of young people about work experience cover the full range from 'Brilliant!' to 'Rubbish!' Sixteen- and 17-year-olds who could reflect on at least two work placements took the overall view that the experience was, on balance, a good idea but could be very variable. They made many practical points which are summarised as follows:

- The Year 10 placement (at 14 or 15 years) can be a bit of a shock. You think it will be a break from school and then you find it's hard and you may even be getting up earlier, to travel to the work.
- Some placements sound very exciting, but you can end up just doing the boring jobs – making tea or photocopying. Especially in a place with strict hygiene or safety rules, they don't let 14-year-olds do anything interesting.
- In a good placement they will let you get involved in different parts of the work and then you learn so much.
- Places will often trust a 17-year-old more, so you can get a better feel of what the job means. If you're keen, they may want to attract you into the job.
- You can be more focused when you know what you want to do, whatever your age.

Working outside school hours

Some young people have part time jobs while they are still at school. This can include weekend, early morning or evening work. Young people can legally get a part time job once they are 13 years of age. However, they cannot work more than two hours within the day, except on Saturday, and their hours must not start before 7.00 a.m. or extend beyond 7.00 p.m. They are not permitted to do any work involving heavy lifting or carrying and there are restrictions about operating machinery.

Young people take jobs delivering papers, stacking shelves in super-markets, washing up in pubs or restaurants and a range of fairly basic jobs. At least in some cases, legal limits and local bye laws are circumvented on hours and type of work. Sometimes the people employing young people are unclear about the law. For instance, there is nothing to prevent parents paying a 14-year-old to baby-sit, and some 14-year-olds are very competent. However, in law, the parents remain responsible for their children, and whatever happens in their absence, if they leave an under 16-year-old in charge.

Young people take these part time jobs for the money. They may incidentally gain some insight into the responsibilities of a job, along with the welcome cash. The money gets spent in different ways, depending on the young people themselves and their families. Some young people are working to fund their leisure time activities or events such as a school trip which parents cannot finance, or not entirely. Others are working to buy large possessions, like bikes, that their families will not buy for them or for a wider range of clothes than their parents will fund. Some young people are working specifically to help their families in a tight financial situation.

Teachers, parents and sometimes the young people themselves are concerned to make sure that the part time work does not impinge on study, either through the number of hours worked or the level of tiredness that results. Young people often find that a part time job, plus the requirements of study in the later years of secondary school and the wish to socialise with friends, are impossible to squeeze into the time available – difficult choices must be made.

Choices in employment

Some young people have a specific career in mind as they work towards qualifications and plan for some kind of further training or education. Some have less specific plans and simply hope for a job that they will find reasonably satisfying and which will pay fairly well.

The employment situation

Many young people are well aware that the economic climate is not favourable and that finding a job may be hard and involve periods of unemployment. In some areas of the country the prospects for young people are very bleak. Some groups, for instance young black people, may find that overt or covert discrimination makes their prospects even slimmer. Young people with disabilities, or continuing health conditions which they need to declare, may also find greater difficulty in being accepted for a job. Some young people may also be wishing to enter a job more traditionally viewed as appropriate for the other sex.

Several points seem to be important in maintaining a positive outlook for any young person and these are listed below. Schools and careers officers often do their part to encourage a realistic and positive approach.

- It is wise for young people to be flexible and to allow for a number of choices, rather than being absolutely set on one kind of job.
- They may not get a job quickly or easily, and may not necessarily get their preferred type of job straightaway. It may be sensible to take what is possible and at least build up some experience and a track record that shows willingness.
- Good self presentation through letter, curriculum vitae and at interview will be crucial when many people are seeking few jobs.
- Young people cannot expect a job for life. Few, if any, jobs are now 'safe'. The whole employment situation is riddled with unpredictability. They need to prepare for a working life that will include changes and probably, for most, some spells of unemployment.
- Young people will need to be able to rethink their skills and the possibilities of what they could do, to be prepared to get different qualifications or take up opportunities for on-the-job training. In their plans and ambitions, flexibility is crucial.
- Young people need up-to-date information. The general pattern has been that, in jobs requiring qualifications, the level of qualification has steadily risen.

Finding a job

Paid work is seen by many – by adults and young people themselves – as one of the symbols of finally growing up. Yet this symbol will not be easily gained by many young people. They may well have experienced the tough realities if one of their parents has been made redundant, perhaps taking some time to find another job. Others may have recognised the stress within their families as parents worry about the risk of becoming unemployed or of keeping the family business viable.

The prospect of unemployment after leaving school and of difficulty in getting a job is a gloomy one for young people. It affects both sexes, although young men may feel their lack especially seriously, since, despite all the general social changes, they still feel that they should be able to support themselves and a family. However, young women do not usually relish the prospect of not being able to earn and many wish to be financially independent.

Despite the extent to which many people complain about their work, having a job gives a structure to life. The prospect of hours of leisure may initially seem very attractive to young people, especially after the restrictions of school and exams. However, leisure time really only has meaning when it is a break from something – work or study. Leisure time is 'time off' and when there is no work to provide the main filler of time young people can feel disoriented. The discomfort is not just due to the lack of money to fund enjoyable leisure activities.

Some unemployed young people create or find more structure in their lives than others:

- Some take whatever job is available, even part time, even one that brings in little more than unemployment benefit.
- Some seek out voluntary work that is close to their preferred kind of job and which will show seriousness as they try to get paid work.
- Some help out in running the household for parents, although this seems to be a task more likely to be given to young women than men.
- Some take up on offers of further courses of study, or training, although these do not guarantee a job.

Some young people, however, tend to drift. As a result they may come into conflict with their families, who are irritated by sons or daughters who hang around at home, sleep late and rarely help out in the household.

Unemployment, especially if it is more than short term, tends to depress young people's self-confidence. Even with full support from their families, they can begin to doubt themselves and their ability to find any work. They may lose the motivation needed to keep trying. A lowered sense of self-esteem may then lead them to make less effort or less effective attempts at self presentation through letter, application form or interview. Their experience of failure to get a job becomes despondency, and risks becoming a self-fulfilling prophecy.

To think about

Paid work provides a sense of identity to many people of all ages. The question, 'What do you do?' is almost always meant to imply, 'What do you get paid for doing?' Having a job and the type of job held is the basis of how many people define themselves and others.

Young people who have completed their studies look for a full entry into the world of work, since this is part of adulthood. If they face unemployment, they not only lose the attraction of earning their own money but also feel that they have not yet gained responsibility for their own life – part of being an adult.

16. Health and well-being of children and young people

Risk taking

Adults responsible for children and young people will probably always worry. Parents, especially, can become very fraught about potential dangers once children and young people are outside their immediate protection. Parents worry about tobacco smoking, under-age or excessive drinking, illegal drug use and sexual activity. Young people's outlook on sex was discussed from page 146; the other issues are covered in this section. Books on development in 'Further reading' have sections on risk taking but a specific source for further reading in this area is Plant and Plant, 1992.

Some older children and many young people are fully aware that their parents worry and to an extent they understand the reasons. The young people's perspective tends to be that parents overdo the worrying, exaggerate the dangers and should trust more in their sons' and daughters' good sense. The two perspectives will never be completely compatible but some compromise may be possible, especially if adults remain sceptical of the more sensational media coverage.

The attraction of risk taking

The years of late childhood and especially of adolescence are a time for experimentation – for pushing back the boundaries and moving into what appears to be more adult behaviour. Young people have more experience and an extended time perspective compared with young children. However, they sometimes do not look very far ahead, at least not in all aspects of their lives. Children and young people may also be unaware of specific risks, for instance the potentially lethal dangers of alcohol poisoning as opposed to getting drunk. Young people are probably more likely to take risks than adults, although there is tremendous variability over tolerance of risk level in every age group.

In matters of health and general well-being, young people can have a sense of near-invulnerability. Given the great improvement in the health of the general population, they may scarcely have encountered serious illness or death in their close circle. The prospect of long-term health risks, such as those associated with smoking, may seem so remote as to be irrelevant if the pressures in their group are pro-tobacco.

In many ways, taking risks or tolerating the uncertainties of taking a chance is part of adolescence and young adulthood. Adults, especially parents and teachers, may not see it this way, yet many everyday activities of young people require them to push out the limits, to try new experiences and to take different types of risks (see page 115).

To think about

Parents understandably worry a great deal about the specific health dangers of drugs and alcohol. Yet, statistics on injury and fatality show that young people are still far more likely to be harmed or killed in an accident, especially a road accident. Admittedly, a proportion of such accidents are caused through the effects of drink or drugs.

The issue of legality

Smoking and drinking are legal activities for adults and young people past a specified age. It is illegal to sell cigarettes to under-16s. But children and young people who smoke do not often appear to have much difficulty in buying them. It is an anomaly that the legal drinking age for children within the home is five years, although they cannot get served in public houses until they are aged 18 years.

Young people and legality

Although tobacco use is legal, a wide range of other drugs such as cannabis or heroin are illegal for anyone. Placing certain drugs beyond the legal boundaries is explained for reasons of health dangers, including the risk of addiction.

This generation of children and young people has experienced strong health education messages, often supported by work in school, on the dangers to short- and long-term health of smoking tobacco and drinking alcohol. Yet, with the clarity of youth, they will point out that tobacco is legal and many adults persevere in smoking despite the evidence. They may well take the same line on alcohol. This generation may therefore see less of a sharp line between legal and illegal narcotics. In fact, some of the drugs information literature includes tobacco and alcohol along with illegal drugs.

Religious conviction

For parents with strong religious convictions the key issues for alcohol, cigarettes or other drugs may not be restricted to health and legality. Part of religious faith for some people is that alcohol is unacceptable in any form. For some people, any kind of stimulant – including caffeine – is inappropriate within a properly ordered life. Children and young people may share and follow their parents' convictions, and the religious framework may give them additional strength to turn down offers. The other possibility, as always with young people, is that a total ban may make the relevant substance that much more attractive.

Alcohol

Studies suggest that the majority of young people in Britain consume alcohol at some point, some on a regular basis, and that during their adolescence they will have at least some experience of mild intoxication and the associated side effects.

Statistics are rarely helpful in making a reliable comparison between the current generation of young people and their parents' behaviour at the same age. Consequently, adults who are ready to worry can conclude that it is this generation of young people which has discovered under-age drinking. Anecdotal evidence, at least, suggests that many of the parents of young people were going into public houses in their mid-teens, and were taking alcohol to parties.

Drinking a large amount of alcohol can be dangerous, especially for children. Evening drinking in particular causes the body to produce insulin the following morning. The condition of low blood sugar (hypoglycaemia) adds to the general unpleasantness of a hangover in adults, but in children this can cause permanent brain damage or death.

Most alcohol-related problems for young people are not the physical consequences of chronic heavy drinking and genuine alcohol dependence. Problems are far more likely to arise from the temporary ill effects of being drunk. For most young people this will involve feeling ill, but there are several serious dangers from heavy drinking sessions for young people. Accidents, sometimes fatal, can occur when young people are intoxicated. They may crash their vehicles, be knocked down when they wander into the road or be injured in falls. If they get extremely drunk and pass out, there is a risk of choking on their own vomit. The risks are multiplied if drugs are taken at the same time. Alcohol poisoning and liver damage can be a serious danger in 'macho' drinking, when young people – more usually young men – drink a large quantity of spirits in a very short space of time.

Illegal drug use

Availability

Previously there was an assumption that young people in cities were particularly likely to be tempted by illegal drugs. But now there is plenty of evidence that young people can get into activities that are potentially dangerous to themselves in small towns and rural areas.

The shift in 1995 in government strategy over anti-drugs campaigns was made in recognition that, unless their families enforce a very

sheltered social life, young people will encounter illegal drugs. This contact is likely to take place in very ordinary social settings and through people they know, sometimes friends. Campaigns against 'drug abusers' and talk about 'war on drugs' were not linked with young people's likely experience of coming across drugs from ordinary people.

Some children and young people use a range of solvents like drugs. Some young people become very ill, or even die, as a result of their use of solvents. However, this type of risk taking does not seem to be as prevalent as illegal drug usage.

Experimentation

The approval of their friends means a great deal to young people and this may be a factor in deciding to experiment with an offer of drugs, or in finding it hard to turn the offer down. The same patterns can be operating over pressure to smoke cigarettes or drink unwise amounts of alcohol.

Many young people are likely to be offered illegal drugs at some time, or to be in a place where drugs are easily available. Most illegal drug use seems to be for straightforward enjoyment, often at parties or dances. However, all young people do not accept what is on offer, neither do those who accept necessarily continue beyond one experimental try.

The Schools Health Education Unit at the University of Exeter reported, on the basis of a substantial survey of young people, that experimenting with cannabis had increased from 1989 to 1993. In 1989 one in 20 of the 15- and 16-year-old boys were saying they had tried cannabis; by 1993 this proportion was closer to one in three. The figures were lower for girls but still showed an increase. However, experimenting with other drugs, such as heroin or cocaine, or knowing someone who had used them was a great deal lower.

The majority of risk taking by young people in this sphere is experienced without major incident. Heavy drug or alcohol users are rather different and tend to have many problems – social, emotional and financial. However, the point soon comes when it can be hard to untangle the likely causes of the shift to addictive behaviour from the consequences of seeking, buying and using the substance.

Smoking tobacco

Cigarette usage is legal for the general population and this situation exists alongside the mounting information on damage to the health of smokers and to those around them. Some young people will justify experimentation with cannabis on the grounds that it is on a par with tobacco. Others dismiss the whole array of drugs – legal and illegal – and are scathing about adults who smoke cigarettes in the face of the health evidence.

Young people are more likely to smoke tobacco if:

- their parents smoke;
- their parents take a permissive line on smoking;
- their best friend smokes;
- they are having a difficult time at school which persists.

Young people are being given some mixed messages over tobacco and their views are perhaps a reflection of this. Some totally reject the possibility of ever smoking and are dismissive of smokers. Yet the more general decline in tobacco smoking in the British population has been far less marked in young people, especially among females. Some young women seem to believe that smoking will act as an appetite depressant, supporting their wish to diet.

Young people are more likely to smoke when their social group equates smoking with looking grown up and a necessary addition to a stylish image. Under these conditions, cigarettes are an appealing prop, but the same attractiveness does not necessarily hold for all social or cultural groups.

In 1995 the National Cancer Institute in the United States released data indicating that the proportion of African-American adolescents who smoked was considerably lower than for white adolescents. A likely explanation seemed to be that African-American community leaders had made great efforts to break the link between cigarettes and assumed maturity, including resisting some poster advertising campaigns in their neighbourhoods. Young African-American women also seemed to be less swayed by the image of super-thin models, so possibly were not attracted to smoking as an appetite depressant.

How can adults help?

Adults close to young people cannot ensure that they will never be tempted by the various legal or illegal substances. Simply telling young people that they must not take drink or drugs is not likely to help. This approach fails to take account of the many pressures to conform that may build up on them. Several, related approaches can help:

- Be well informed about drink and drugs, but also try to appreciate the way that young people may see the issues, for instance, whether there is a neat and justifiable line of legality.
- Be prepared to talk with children and young people. It will be far less helpful if this is pushed into one long conversation. There will usually be a wide range of opportunities to talk about different potentially risky activities as the topics arise throughout childhood and into adolescence. These include television programmes (dramas, regular series including the 'soaps' and documentaries), health education at school, leaflets or useful books.

- It is better not to delay introducing the topic until circumstances have provoked anxiety. Adults, especially parents, in a high state of worry do not usually manage very useful conversations with young people.

Viewpoint

A group of 13-year-olds showed a high awareness of parents' worries, but were generally uncomfortable about having a serious conversation thrust upon them. One young woman summed up the view of the group with:

'Parents have such pressure from the media. They see and read these things and they get so worried about what you're exposed to. They try to trust you but they want to protect you. Then they think they should talk to you about drugs.'

- Conversations, at a suitable time when young people are in the mood to talk, should be as much adults' listening as talking. What do the young people themselves think, what do they know, what do their friends think?
- There may be opportunities at other times to talk over generally the feelings of pressure – being pushed into something by friends, or finding it hard to be the one who stands out.

None of the above works well unless young people feel part of a two-way conversation and wish to talk. It is important to ask for their opinions, rather than telling them what to do and what not to do, and vital to treat their answers with respect. Conversations about matters that worry adults are more likely to be tolerated by young people if they have plenty of experience that the adults will respect them for their efforts to keep healthy and on the legal side of the boundaries. Young people often stress how adults should trust them, so it is worth taking every possible opportunity to treat older children and young people as if they were responsible individuals.

Finally, it is both sensible and reasonable to have ground rules about alcohol and drugs, including tobacco, for a family home or a shared facility as such an after-school club. Adults should expect the rules to be followed and have a clear idea of what is to happen if somebody breaks a rule. Young people can, in their turn, expect a good example to be set by the adults involved.

Physical health and well-being

In Britain during the twentieth century, the mortality rate of young people under the age of 20 years has fallen by over 90 per cent. The serious killers such as cholera, typhoid, tuberculosis or diphtheria are no longer a real hazard in the Western hemisphere, although they are part of life, and death, in many parts of the world. So, children and young people in Britain are far more likely to survive to adulthood than their counterparts in the nineteenth or, even, early twentieth centuries.

Accidents

Although some individuals' health and life is threatened by illness, the greater risk for most children and young people is from accidental injury and death. (The figures that follow are taken from Woodruffe and others, 1993.)

Injuries and poisoning are the cause of 37 per cent of the deaths of five- to nine-year-olds, 39 per cent of ten- to 14-year-olds and 60 per cent of 15- to 19-year-olds. Eighty per cent of the fatal injuries are accidental. There are risks in the home, often from the wealth of potentially dangerous household gadgets. However, unlike younger children, the over-eights are more likely to come into danger outside their home, overwhelmingly from road traffic.

At all ages, and for most types of accident, boys are more likely to be involved in an accidental injury than girls. For instance, in 1990 two-thirds of the pedestrian casualties were boys. Over five times as many boys as girls were killed or seriously injured in bicycle accidents. There are two likely reasons for this:

1. Parents seem, on balance, to be more willing to let their sons out on their own than their daughters.
2. Boys seem to be more vulnerable than girls, on average, to the lure of physical dares. Turning down a dare, even a patently unsafe challenge, is viewed by some – possibly many – boys as a threat to their self-esteem.

This pattern continues into young adulthood. For instance, in 1990, of the motorbike, scooter and moped riders aged under 20 involved in such accidents, 90 per cent were young men. This statistic has to be interpreted bearing in mind that male riders of two-wheeled vehicles do outnumber female. However, the imbalance holds for car accidents too. In 1990, of the 33,166 car drivers under 20 years of age who were involved in a road accident with a resulting injury, nearly three-quarters were young men rather than young women.

Parents, or anyone else responsible for young people, are in an unenviable position. They can work hard in the earlier years to coach children in safer ways of behaving, specific learning about road safety and in an awareness of general risks, including those within the home. However, as described in other sections of the book (page 12 and page 108) part of growing up is that children and young people increasingly operate without a supervising adult.

Perhaps one of the most practical steps for parents to take over the road accident statistics is to stress the importance of not riding with a driver who is known to be irresponsible behind the handlebars or wheel, or who is clearly the worse for alcohol. If feasible, the willingness to pick up one's son or daughter by car, or provide taxi money, are other practical options.

Continuing health conditions

Some parents will have been caring for children whose health condition has been evident from the early years. Others will be facing, with their children or young people, the onset of a condition that is new – for instance, the start of hay fever and other allergies, or late onset diabetes. Some young people may experience a new set of frustrations with an existing condition, as they wish to establish an independent social life and fret at the restrictions or medical requirements of their condition.

Death from serious illness has reduced dramatically for children and young people. However, some specific chronic illnesses in the under-sixteens age group have been increasing over the last 20 years in Britain – for instance, respiratory diseases such as asthma, and diabetes. In 1990, 14 per cent of under-sixteens had a long standing illness and three per cent a defined disability. The reasons for the increases are not certain but pollution seems one likely cause. Environmental pollution is likely to affect the general well-being of all children and young people, but will be more swiftly experienced by those who already have respiratory problems such as asthma.

Disruptions caused by ill-health

Continuing health conditions can affect children's whole lives and influence their view of themselves. Frequent periods of hospitalisation or time off school at home because of illness can be very disruptive of a child's education. Parents and hospital support staff can lessen the educational impact by helping children to continue with their studies as much as possible. The social side of school and friendships remain an issue for children and young people, who may feel as badly about trying to re-enter the social scene as about catching up with missed work. Parents can help by, as far as possible, making it easy for friends to visit. A very practical gesture is to tolerate a higher telephone bill, as their son or daughter keeps in touch with friends and acquaintances.

In a similar pattern to that of adjusting to disabilities, children with a permanent or recurring health condition may need additional support from their family as they get older. Older children can become very self-conscious, perhaps more so than when they were younger, as the difference they perceive between themselves and others of their age becomes, in their eyes, more marked. Young people may become resistant to taking medication or wish to find a way to achieve this very discreetly. They may well experience a new set of frustrations as they feel that their health is blocking the kind of more independent social life that their peers seem to be managing with considerably less effort or need for forward planning.

Parents, and teachers, have a responsibility to support children in building and holding on to a positive self-image that does not leave them defined entirely through their health condition. This kind of support has to be a continuing pattern of communication. The worries or upset of generally confident children and young people may be triggered unexpectedly by unkind comments from other children or the intolerance of adults who do not understand the condition.

Children, young people and the health services

Medical decisions and consent

When they reach 16 years of age, young people in Britain are judged to be capable of making their own medical decisions and have the right to confidentiality in their consultations.

This development can happen at a younger age, since there is a general principle at work in law that children have the right to make decisions for themselves once they are judged to be of 'sufficient understanding'. The principle also upholds the concept that parents' rights exist only for the benefit of the child, not that of the parent, and are justified only in order for parents to fulfil their duties to their children. This principle emerged from the case brought by Victoria Gillick in 1980 in a failed attempt to establish the precedent that doctors could not prescribe the contraceptive pill to under-sixteens without parents' knowledge and consent.

Yet the legal position remains uncertain and may be challenged in the courts when there is dissent between parents and young people over a medical decision. What has come to be known as the 'Gillick principle' has not been made part of written law but does have weight in case law, though it has been challenged by later court cases.

Difficult dilemmas can and do arise when the parents' preferred decision is contrary to the apparent preference of a child or young person, or is dangerous to their well-being. For instance, deeply held beliefs against the giving or receiving of blood among Jehovah's Witnesses have led to medical conflict. Some cases have gone to court to challenge a decision by parents which would almost certainly lead to the death of a child who did not receive a transfusion.

Good practice in dealing with children and young people

Many medical decisions are not at a life threatening level. Within family life, part of growing up is that older children and young people steadily move towards making and keeping their own appointments. The kinds of visits for which they want the company of a parent may reduce; they are able to deal with their own visits to the doctor, dentist or optician.

Viewpoint

One 12-year-old explained how she did not mind going to the optician:

'She's very nice and she listens to what I say. It's like she's really interested in my eyes. The time that I am in with her, I get all this attention, just for me. It makes me feel really special.'

Parents can work to support their children's confidence and learn to stand back as a son or daughter takes over the main part of a conversation with a health professional. For this to work, of course, the health professionals themselves have to communicate well with children and young people, along with their parents. Health services have some staff who are respectful and informative in their dealings with younger users of the service. Some staff are not pleasant but they may well also be dismissive and unforthcoming with adults, possibly because of negative general attitudes to people defined as 'patients'.

The key points of good practice for health care professionals in dealing with children and young people are not so very different from good communication with adults:

- Children and young people should be allowed to speak for themselves and professionals should listen to what they say.
- Recognise young people's feelings and their right to make decisions.

Viewpoint

One mother explained how her own childhood experience had made her sensitive to the feelings of her children as they went through orthodontic work:

'I will never forget the dentist who looked at my teeth. She didn't say a word to me, she just talked to my father. And then I spoke up and said that I wasn't at all sure I wanted to wear a brace. She still looked at my father and said, "What does she care? She's only 15. She's too young to care how she looks."'

- Acknowledge their pain, distress, embarrassment and, sometimes, sheer boredom of waiting or going through medical procedures.
- Young people need information. Adults can get confused, especially under stress or shock, but have a broader experience in which to place it. Children and young people need honest information, probably communicated more than once, and a chance to ask questions when they are ready.
- Some adults want to believe that children and young people cannot

understand issues that the adults themselves would rather not voice. The panic that can arise from ignorance is usually a greater risk for children than being upset by information.

- Children and young people want personal respect, privacy and a sense of dignity just as much as adults. These feelings are shared by all but may be especially sharp within some cultures, perhaps requiring that a same-sex professional deals with the case.

Hospital procedures with children and young people have changed over the last 30 years. Compared with the 1950s, for instance, parents are far more welcome on the wards and viewed as important to their children's recovery, rather than a source of intrusion and infection.

It is a measure of the change that Action for Sick Children now produces a short publication about children who are not accompanied into hospital by a parent. It is now regarded as normal practice that parents, or another close relative, will be actively involved, probably staying in the hospital with the child or young person, and accompanying them right up to the moment when they go for final anaesthetic.

Health in the family

Recent approaches in health psychology have stressed that illness or disability are not simply a process of physical and physiological factors. Nor is it accurate to see a child or young person who is ill as a single individual passively reacting to a given condition or accident. When any child or young person is ill, there will be reverberations within the whole family.

Parents are dealing with the health of the child who is ill, but also with everyone's feelings and worries. Having a seriously ill or disabled child or young person has an impact, not only on parents but also on brothers and sisters. Their possible family life is changed. Siblings may have less of their parents' time and attention than, ideally, they would like. They may feel obligated, even if willingly, to help out with the household tasks or other parts of family life, including care of their brother or sister.

Children and young people can also be very distressed about the well-being and future prospects of a very ill or disabled sibling. Some units that care for children and young people are concerned to make time and speak with other children in the family, to involve them in what is happening and to be honest with them.

Final thoughts

Any adults closely involved over a matter of years with young children cannot help but realise the wide-ranging changes that occur as those children develop. The adults themselves have little choice but to adjust as children's physical skills grow, along with their powers of communication and their understanding of the world around them.

There are just as many developments occurring as girls and boys move through late childhood as in adolescence, when a visibly more obvious set of changes, released through the process of puberty, occurs. Adults who are concerned to support children and young people need to be prepared to make adjustments themselves, to the same extent, although not in exactly the same way, as had to be done when much younger children made the striking moves into easy mobility or understandable language.

The world of children and young people is one shared with adults, but it is not experienced in the same way by the different age groups, nor will subsequent generations' experience be exactly the same. Some adults are swift to claim that children or young people do not appreciate the complexities or burdens of an adult life. But, it can be claimed, with as much justification, that some adults fail to offer in exchange a whole-hearted attempt to grasp what life is like for children and young people – the enjoyable times as well as the difficulties.

The different sections of this book have covered not only the kinds of changes happening within development for older children and young people, but what these can mean from their perspective. Adults – any adults closely involved with younger people – can be a far more helpful support if they have a sound understanding of development, as well as an abiding concern for children and young people.

It is probably inevitable that the effort to look through the eyes of children and young people will bring uncomfortable realisations to adults, as well as real interest and pleasure. It can prompt an understanding, surprising to some adults, of how carefully younger people think over some issues. They consider matters sometimes from another angle to adults, and occasionally with an emotional power that takes adults by surprise. However, their perspectives are valid and often can provide the essential addition to adult viewpoints, if difficulties are to be resolved or children's welfare is to be considered in a meaningful way.

A detailed survey of the changes that may be unfolding in the development of older children and young people can offer a sobering reminder of what is possible. Sometimes, for various reasons, children and young people are not stretching themselves or reaching out towards their true potential, and this can be a matter for serious concern. However, the sweeping changes in their development are also a timely reminder that intellectual skills, or a grasp of social or moral issues, are not applied in a neat and predictable way.

There were instances in this book when it seemed very important to point out that adults do not always behave in a logical or sensible manner, nor do they always make full use of their talents or their time. So it is utterly unreasonable for them to expect higher and unrealistic standards of children or young people.

Perhaps the continuity of development between childhood and into adulthood is one of the most important themes for any adult to retain and apply in everyday life. Children and young people often do have another perspective; they have some different interests and pressing concerns when a direct comparison is made with adults. However, they are steadily moving towards adulthood and many of them are very aware of the changes they have experienced so far, as well as what is yet to come.

Much of what older children and young people ask of adults bears some relation to the whole process of growing up, as well as their immediate concerns at their current age. They ask for support – often recognising that adults, especially parents, have difficulty in getting it right all the time – and respect for their obligations and point of view. Without wishing for an utterly serious life, older children and young people ask that their perspective and their concerns be taken seriously. There can be a very great deal for adults to learn, a lot of interest and some genuine pleasure, if they will give time and attention to this task.

Further reading

The books suggested for further reading are available from book shops or libraries. Details of any booklets published by organisations include their address for enquiry about availability and current price.

Bee, Helen (seventh edition, 1994) *The developing child*. Harper Collins.
Thorough coverage of children's development from birth to adolescence. A good source for a balanced discussion of sex differences in development, and for cultural differences.

Carter, Margaret (1989) *You and your child in hospital*. Methuen.
A practical book for families whose child will be spending time in hospital.

Central Statistics Office (1992) *Social Trends*, 22 HMSO

Children's Legal Centre (1995) *At what age can I?*
Booklet detailing the legal position on different activities for children and young people. Contact the Centre at the University of Essex, Wivenhoe Park, Colchester, Essex CO4 3SQ, tel: 01206 873820.

Children's Rights Office (1995) *Building small democracies: respecting children's civil rights within the family. The implications of the UN Convention*. Children's Rights Office.
Information and explanation of the UN convention and areas of children's rights. The Children's Rights Office can be contacted at 235 Shaftesbury Avenue, London WC2 H 8EL, tel: 0171 240 4499.

Cobb, Nancy J (1992) *Adolescence – continuity, change and diversity*. US, California: Mayfield Publishing Company.
The information is more based on the United States experience but is still useful for growing up in Britain.

Coleman, John C and Hendry, Leo (second edition, 1990) *The nature of adolescence*. Routledge.
A source for reading more about theory and research on the years of adolescence.

Coleman, John C (1995) *Teenagers and sexuality*. Trust for the Study

of Adolescence/Hodder and Stoughton.
A handbook for parents dealing with a range of practical issues as young people become more sexually aware.

Council for Disabled Children (1996) *A resource book for parents of children and young people with disabilities from the age of 10–18 years.* Council for Disabled Children.
Practical information on services and legislation. Available from the Council for Disabled Children, 8 Wakley Street, London EC1V 7QE, tel: 0171 843 6058.

Cruse (1993) *Caring for bereaved children.* Cruse.
One of a number of leaflets published by Cruse, the bereavement care charity. Contact them for current publications list at 126 Sheen Road, Richmond, Surrey, TW9 1UR, tel: 0181 940 4818.

De'Ath, Erica (1990) *Teenagers growing up in a stepfamily.* Stepfamily Publications.
De'Ath, Erica (1993), *A baby of our own, a new baby in a stepfamily.* Stepfamily Publications.
Both these practical booklets are available, with other publications, from Stepfamily Publications, Chapel House, 18 Hatton Place, London EC1N 8RU, tel: 0171 209 2460.

Eiser, C (1993) *Growing up with a chronic disease: the impact on children and their families.* Jessica Kingsley.
This book recognises the distress for families in caring for a very sick or disabled child, but also covers ways of coping in families.

Elliott, Michele (1991) *Bullying – a practical guide to coping in schools.* Longman/Kidscape.
A collection of articles about aspects of dealing with bullying in school situations.

Epilepsy and the young adult (1994). *Epilepsy and the young adult.* EYA.
A practical booklet from the EYA; a good example of answering the kind of questions that are asked by young people with a continuing health condition. The booklet is available from EYA, 13 Crondace Road, London SW6 4BB, tel: 0171 736 0123.

Fenwick, Elizabeth and Smith, Tony (1993) *Adolescence – the survival guide for parents and teenagers.* Dorling Kindersley.
An easily consulted book, with sections written for young people themselves. Full of information and sound advice, including medical.

Fowler, Deborah (1993) *A guide to adoption – the other road to parenthood.* Optima.
Practical information about the process of adoption, as well as discussion of the feelings involved.

Fowler, Deborah (1992) *Loving other people's children*. Vermilion.
A book about the practicalities of stepfamilies, including some personal accounts.

Graham, Laurie (1992) *Teenagers – a family survival guide*. Chatto and Windus.
A personal and very readable account of living with teenagers, including practical advice.

Grieve, Robert and Hughes, Martin eds (1990) *Understanding children*. Basil Blackwell.
A collection of articles on different aspects of how children learn and grow in understanding.

Hardyment, Christina (1995) *Perfect parents*. Oxford University Press.
A book that looks at some of the myths as well as the information about families.

Hartley–Brewer, Elizabeth (1994) *Positive parenting – raising children with self–esteem*. Mandarin.
Discussion of ideas and action in taking an encouraging approach to children and young people within the family, but equally applicable to any adults working with children.

Hudson, Frances and Ineichen, Bernard (1991) *Taking it lying down: sexuality and teenage motherhood*. Macmillan.
A review of research and studies of teenage motherhood, including some personal accounts.

Humphries, Steve (1988) *A secret world of sex – forbidden fruit: the British experience 1900–1950*. Sidgwick and Jackson.
Humphries, S and Gordon, P (1993) *A labour of love: the experience of parenthood in Britain 1900–1950*. Sidgwick and Jackson.
Both of Steve Humphries' books are helpful in gaining a historical perspective on families, children and young people. The personal accounts that he uses through his oral history approach are particularly effective in showing the realities of life for previous generations.

Ives, Richard ed. (1989) *Sniffing solutions: Young people, drugs and solvents*. National Children's Bureau.
Information and some personal accounts from young people.

Jeffree, Dorothy and Cheseldine, Sally (1984) *Let's join in*. Human Horizons Series, Souvenir Press.
A very practical book, full of ideas for play and leisure activities for older children and young people with disabilities.

Keirsey, David and Bates, Marilyn (1984) *Please understand me*. Oxford Psychologists Press.
Informative about personality styles and how these affect children, young people and adults in their relationships with others.

Konner, Melvin (1991) *Childhood*. Little Brown and Company/Channel 4 Publications.
The book that accompanied the television series – a useful source of information on growing up around the world.

Lansdown, Richard (1980) *More than sympathy – the everyday needs of sick and handicapped children*. Tavistock.
Written from experience at the Great Ormond Street Hospital, this book combines information and empathy with families.

Lawrence, Gordon D (1993) *People types and tiger stripes*. Oxford Psychologists Press.
Written for teachers, but helpful for anyone concerned with children and young people, the book shows how personality style affects how everyone learns.

Lindon, Jennie (1996) *Help your child with homework and exams*. Hodder and Stoughton.
Practical information and suggestions on how parents can help their children, as they pass through the years of secondary school – grounded in how children and young people learn.

Lindon, Jennie and Lindon, Lance (1993) *Your child from 5–11*. Hodder and Stoughton.
Suggestions on supporting children through late childhood, with particular emphasis on communication within the family and learning self–reliance.

Lindon, Jennie and Lindon, Lance (1994, updated edition 1995) *Help your child through school*. Hodder and Stoughton.
Practical advice and information for children and their families through the primary school years and into the beginning of secondary.

Lovell, Anne (1995) *When your child comes out*. Sheldon Press.
A practical book, written for parents but equally helpful to any adults concerned for young people finding their sexual orientation, and for their families. Through personal accounts, the book gives a sense of the great variety of reactions from parents and the experience of young people themselves.

Miedzian, Myriam (1992) *Boys will be boys – breaking the link between masculinity and violence*. Virago.
Thought-provoking and informative book about the pressures on boys and young men as well as critical of social norms that value aggression.

Moore, Susan and Rosenthal, Doreen (1993) *Sexuality in adolescence*. Routledge.
A review of research on the sexual development of young people.

Murgatroyd, Stephen and Woolfe, Ray (1985) *Helping families in distress: an introduction to family focussed helping*. Harper and Row.
Discussion of families that manage well and those that experience difficulties, along with approaches to helping families in conflict.

Phoenix, Ann, Woollett, Anne and Lloyd, Eva eds (1991) *Motherhood: meanings, practice and ideologies*. Sage.
A collection of articles looking at research and ideas in the approach to the experience of motherhood.

Plant, Martin and Plant, Moira (1992) *Risk–takers – alcohol, drugs, sex and youth*. Tavistock/Routledge.
A review of different risk-taking behaviours of young people.

Pugh, Gillian, De'Ath, Erica and Smith, Celia (1994) *Confident parents, confident children: policy and practice in parent education and support*. National Children's Bureau.
A survey of the different kinds of support for parents, the ideas underlying different approaches and the current gaps in service.

Quilliam, Susan (1994) *Child watching: a parent's guide to children's body language*. Ward Lock.
Written for parents, but equally relevant for any adults who spend time with children and young people.

Russell, Philippa (1994) *The transition to adult life: parents' views*.
A paper on parents' perspectives as their children with disabilities grow towards adulthood. Available from the Council for Disabled Children, 8 Wakley Street, London EC1V 7QE, tel: 0171 843 6058.

Russell, Philippa (1996) *Partnership with parents: the transition to adult life*. National Children's Bureau.

Sandbank, Audrey (1988) *Twins and the family*. Tamba.
This book and other publications on twins and multiple births in the family are available from Tamba, 17 Clevedon Green, South Littleton, Evesham, Worcs. WR11 5TY.

Schaffer, H. Rudolf (1990) *Making decisions about children – psychological questions and answers*. Blackwell.
A balanced commentary on available research shows how often studies lead more to 'it depends...' rather than 'this is the answer'.

Schools Health Education Unit (1995) *Young people in 1994*. SHEU.
The Unit publishes annual reports on the basis of large-scale surveys of 11- to 18-year-olds. Contact the Unit at the University of Exeter, Heavitree Road, Exeter EX1 2LU, tel: 01392 264722.

Sharpe, Sue (1976) *Just like a girl: how girls learn to be women*. Penguin.
This publication is 20 years old, but unfortunately much of it still rings true.

Slater, Mary (1993) *Health for all our children – achieving appropriate health care for black and minority ethnic children.* Action for Sick Children.
Contact address is Argyle House, 29–31 Euston Road, London NW1 2SD, tel: 0171 833 2041.

Smith, Peter M and Berridge, David (1993) *Ethnicity and child care placements.* National Children's Bureau.
Discussion of adoption with particular reference to whether adoptive parents should be of the same ethnic group as the children.

Steinberg, Laurence and Levine, Ann (1992) *You and your adolescent – a parent's guide for ages 10–20.* Vermilion.
Informative about all aspects of adolescents in the family.

Sugarman, Leonie (1986) *Life span development: concepts, theories and interventions.* Methuen.
A view of development as unfolding throughout the entire life span.

Tizard, Barbara and Phoenix, Ann (1993) *Black, white or mixed race? Race and racism in the lives of young people with mixed parentage.* Routledge.
A study of children and young people of mixed parentage, some of whom were adopted. The voices of the children and young people are given equal space with adult perspectives on the topic.

Troyna, Barry and Hatcher, Richard (1992) *Racism in children's lives – a study of mainly white primary schools.* Routledge and the National Children's Bureau.
Research into the views and behaviour of children in the later years of primary school – highlights the frequency of racist name-calling and the complexities of an effective approach to dealing with racism in schools.

Whaite, Anne and Ellis, Judy (1987) *From me to you – advice for parents of children with special needs.* Williams and Wilkins.
An informative and sympathetic book, written from experience, about dealing with other people and the various services when you have a child with special needs.

Woodruffe, Caroline and others (1993) *Children, teenagers and health – the key data.* Open University Press.
A reliable source of statistical information. By the nature of collecting and analysing data, many of the figures are for 1990 or 1991.

INDEX

Publications

Recent works include:

Balancing the Act

Social Work and Assessment with Adolescents

Good Practice in Sex Education: A sourcebook for schools

Children's Rights and HIV

Managing to Change

Schools' SEN Policies Pack

Crossing the Boundaries

Children sex education and the law

It's Your Meeting!

Intervention in the Early Years

The Bureau also publishes a quarterly journal, *Children & Society* – to subscribe please contact John Wiley & Sons,
Tel: 01243 770634 Fax: 01243 770638

For further information or a catalogue please contact:
Book Sales, National Children's Bureau, 8 Wakley Street,
London EC1V 7QE
Tel: 0171 843 6029 Fax: 0171 278 9512